ARRANGING CUT FL

Created and designed by the editorial staff of ORTHO Books.

Project Editor	Deni W. Stein
Writer	Alvin Horton
Designer	Jacqueline Jones
Photographer	Kathryn Kleinman
Photographic stylist	Sara Slavin
Illustrator	Katherine Williamson

Ortho Books

Publisher
Robert L. Iacopi

Editorial Director
Min S. Yee

Managing Editors
Anne Coolman
Michael D. Smith
Sally W. Smith

Production Manager
Ernie S. Tasaki

Editors
Jim Beley
Susan Lammers
Deni Stein

System Manager
Christopher Banks

System Consultant
Mark Zielinski

Asst. System Managers
Linda Bouchard
William F. Yusavage

Photographic Director
Alan Copeland

Photographers
Laurie A. Black
Richard A. Christman

Asst. Production Manager
Darcie S. Furlan

Associate Editors
Richard H. Bond
Alice E. Mace

Production Editors
Don Mosley
Kate O'Keeffe

Chief Copy Editor
Rebecca Pepper

Photo Editors
Anne Pederson
Pam Peirce

National Sales Manager
Garry P. Wellman

Sales Associate
Susan B. Boyle

Operations Director
William T. Pletcher

Operations Assistant
Gail L. Davis

Administrative Assistant
Georgiann Wright

Address all inquiries to
Ortho Books
Chevron Chemical Company
Consumer Products Division
575 Market Street
San Francisco, CA 94105

Copyright © 1985
Chevron Chemical Company
All rights reserved under
international and Pan-American
copyright conventions.

First Printing in April, 1985

1 2 3 4 5 6 7 8 9
85 86 87 88 89

ISBN 0-89721-041-7

Library of Congress Catalog Card
Number 85-060007

CONSULTANTS

T.G. Byrne, Floriculturist
Dept. of Environmental Horticulture
University of California
Davis, CA

Alisa A. de Jong-Stout, A.I.F.D.
El Cerrito, CA

Holly Money, A.I.F.D.
San Francisco City College
San Francisco, CA

Soho Sakai
Richmond, CA

Bill Taylor, A.I.F.D.
Sonoma, CA

ACKNOWLEDGMENTS:

(Names of designers and photographers are followed by the page numbers on which their work appears.)

Floral Designs:

A Bed of Roses, Florist, San Francisco, CA: 61

Barbara Belloli, Fioridella, San Francisco, CA: 13, 75

Bloomers, San Francisco, CA: Cover, title page, 10, 17, 59, 70, 72, 82

Alisa A. de Jong-Stout, El Cerrito, CA: 62, 91

Fiegel, Greene and Gypson, San Francisco, CA: 8

Jerry Gillam, The Greenery, San Francisco, CA: 71

Kathleen Holming, Wisteria, Berkeley, CA: 84

Michael Labri, Flowers on the Hill, San Francisco, CA: 14, 15

James McNair, Crystal Bay, NV: 12, 16

Holly Money, A.I.F.D., San Francisco, CA: 51, 56

Ron Morgan, Ron Morgan Custom Floral Design, Piedmont, CA: 7, 11

Regula, Regula's European Design in Flowers, San Francisco, CA: 87

Soho Sakai, Richmond, CA: 78, 79

Jean Thompson, Fioridella, San Francisco, CA: 76

David P. Turner and John G. Martin, Distinctive Floral Impressions, San Mateo, CA: 58, 68, 81

Interior Designs:

Michael Anthony & Assoc., San Francisco, CA: 13

Fiegel, Greene and Gypson, San Francisco, CA: 8

Ted Gietzen, Fabric Walls, Fairfax, CA: 14, 15

Richard Kaleh, Richard Kaleh & Assoc., San Francisco and La Jolla, CA: 61

paper white ltd., Fairfax, CA: 14, 15

Additional Photography:

Michael Landis: 22 (top), 24 (bottom), 32 (top), 36 (bottom)

Michael McKinley: 20, 24 (top), 26 (middle, bottom), 28 (bottom), 30 (middle, bottom), 34 (top)

Pam Peirce: 24 (middle), 26 (top), 28 (top), 30 (top), 34 (bottom)

Bouquet of Flowers on a Ledge, by Jan van Huysum. Courtesy of the J. Paul Getty Museum: 6

Special Thanks To:

Bob Bell, The Greenery, San Francisco, CA
Jeanie Cahill, Oakland, CA
California Evergreen Nurseries, San Francisco, CA
Daniel Campbell, Berkeley, CA
Terri Driscoll, San Francisco, CA
Flowers Faire, San Francisco, CA
Bruno Fournier, Star Dried Flowers B.V./Florado, Paris, France
Tom Gallagher, Perfect Petals, Oakland, CA
Sue Fisher King, San Francisco, CA
Elinor Lindheimer, Ukiah, CA
Neve Wholesale Florists, San Francisco, CA
Orchard Nursery and Florist, Lafayette, CA
The Planters Nursery, San Francisco, CA
Roger Raiche, Berkeley, CA
Dr. Rayford D. Redell, San Francisco, CA
Myrtle R. Wolf, Berkeley, CA
Barbara Worl, Palo Alto, CA

Front Cover Photograph:

An informal arrangement of freesia, rose, cosmos, phlox, foxglove, and other garden flowers.

Back Cover Photograph: Materials for arrangements vary from tender exotics available only from a florist, such as anthurium and protea, to more traditional gladiolus and miniature carnation that can be garden-grown.

Title Page Photograph: This opulent bouquet, including Queen Anne's lace, zinnias, belladonna lilies, roses, and grasses, suggests the bounty of summer.

Chevron Chemical Company
575 Market Street, San Francisco, CA 94105

ARRANGING CUT FLOWERS

POSSIBILITIES UNLIMITED
Flowers can be part of our lives in many ways, from the celebration of holidays, the seasons, and special occasions to the decoration and enhancement of any spot in our homes.
5

FLOWERS FOR ARRANGEMENTS
You can grow your own flowers, purchase them from a florist, or gather them from fields and roadsides— a combination of all three methods will provide you with a rich assortment of materials for arrangements.
19

TOOLS AND TECHNIQUES
Learning the proper techniques and using the proper tools will ensure beautiful, long-lasting arrangements.
41

DESIGNING WITH FLOWERS
Incorporating some basic design principles into your own floral designs will benefit even the simplest of arrangements.
59

A GALLERY OF ARRANGEMENTS
A series of diverse arrangements with a detailed analysis of design, materials, and mechanics is accompanied by suggestions for interesting variations.
71

Left as they are, long-stemmed red florist roses are classic flowers for arrangements. When shortened and combined with other flowers, they offer numerous possibilities to the imaginative arranger.

POSSIBILITIES UNLIMITED

From simple bouquets to elaborate formal arrangements, cut flowers help us celebrate life's events—holidays and important special occasions as well as casual dinner parties. As part of everyday life, flowers are wonderfully decorative, and can brighten any room in the house.

Cut flowers make their mark on our lives in innumerable ways, gracing the simplest of moments to the grandest of occasions. A handful of daisies dropped into a drinking glass brightens a breakfast nook. Garlands, bouquets, corsages, nosegays, altarpieces, and other arrangements set the festive tone of a wedding. An arrangement of glowing red and orange chrysanthemums and brilliant autumn foliage adds warmth to a study. A bowl of summer perennials flanked by candles decorates a dinner table, and a small bouquet brings color and fragrance to a bedside table. A florist's box of red roses arrives at the door of someone's beloved. A birth, a death, an illness, or an anniversary elicit flowers from the community. Cut flowers punctuate our public and private lives. Why? What is their powerful appeal?

The answers are many: Flowers raise our spirits by gratifying our senses with their colors, forms, and fragrances; flowers, with their many pleasing qualities, are convenient, appropriate expressions of happiness, caring, and affection; flowers are a living connection with the natural world. In the end, however, the allure of flowers defies simple explanation.

Cut flowers, universally a favorite household adornment, are enjoying a dramatic upsurge in popularity. This book will lead you on a thorough exploration of ideas and methods for using cut flowers in your home. It is helpful to begin this exploration with a historical perspective.

A Brief History of Cut Flowers

The discovery of a Neanderthal burial site in Iraq with pollen from ornamental flowers such as grape hyacinth and hollyhock has pushed the history of the use of cut flowers back to around 50,000 B.C. Another Neanderthal burial site, dating from around 20,000 B.C., contained a garland of flowers. No further evidence of cut flowers exists from that time until the second and first millenia B.C., when Egyptians wore garlands of flowers on their heads and placed water lilies and lotus blossoms in jars, and foliage with various blossoms in bowls. Ancient Greeks used flowers to make garlands, usually for religious ceremonies and festivals. The Romans adopted many of the Greek uses of flowers; they also covered the floors of their banquet halls with roses and adorned the interiors of their houses with bouquets of flowers.

While the Greeks and Romans were using cut flowers for both religious and secular purposes, Buddhist priests in China and Korea began to develop sophisticated styles of flower arranging. Later, after their adoption and further evolution in Japan, these styles became known as *ikebana*, meaning "arrangement of living plant materials." Ikebana became widely practiced as both a secular and a religious art, though in its secular forms it adhered, and still adheres, to symbolism rooted in a

A casual, spontaneous-looking arrangement of anemones and other garden flowers in an earthenware crock suits its intimate, rustic setting.

Bouquet of Flowers on a Ledge, by Jan van Huysum, one of the best known of the Dutch Old Masters.

religious view. A characteristic of many Japanese designs is their linear form: Straight, curved, or angular lines of vegetation balance the bold use of open space between the lines or masses of plant material. Throughout the centuries, hundreds of schools of ikebana have developed. Two examples of ikebana are shown and discussed on pages 78 and 79.

In northern Europe, it was not until the Renaissance that formal flower arranging became commonplace. Many styles developed, most of them variations on the bouquet (from old French, meaning "clump of trees" or "thicket," referring to the bouquet's solid, massed form). To this day, the bouquet remains the dominant style of arrangement in Europe and the United States. Among the painters of flowers and flower arrangements were the so-called Old Masters of Flanders and Holland, whose fanciful canvases depicted each element of the arrangement in painstaking detail. Flowers, leaves, berries and fruit, and often butterflies, caterpillars, and other insects were carefully rendered. The Old Masters created new styles of floral design as much as they reflected actual practice. Their influence on flower arranging is still very much alive today. See pages 72 and 73 for an example of an arrangement inspired by the Old Masters.

Direct influence on American floral design has come mainly through Great Britain. British styles have ranged from the decorously symmetrical Georgian designs to the effusive but often fussy and rule-bound Victorian designs. Earlier in this century, the famous English designer Constance Spry developed a simpler, more inventive style that sometimes incorporated linear elements of ikebana into the massed form of the bouquet. Without abandoning tradition, she practiced and encouraged a revolutionary concept: originality in flower arranging. "I do feel so strongly," she said, "that flowers should be a medium of self-expression for everyone." Compared with her designs, many modern floral designs are much simpler and less bound to traditional precepts. Still, it was she who made them possible.

What Is a Flower Arrangement?

What is the difference between an arrangement and a handful of flowers dropped into a container? Nothing—if the person who chooses and places the flowers has a keen instinctive or trained awareness of what he or she is doing. A floral arrangement can be a grand, studied construction in a silver urn, with elaborate underpinnings concealed beneath voluminous blossoms and foliage. It can also be a handful of flowers—even a single, carefully selected and positioned blossom—that harmonizes with its container and surroundings to make a spark or create a mood. But a real arrangement is never haphazard, no matter how simple and unstudied it might appear at first glance.

Look on the following page at the three stems of allium in the bathroom setting. Artless as the arrangement might seem at first, it works: The long, slightly curved stems reflect the grooves in the container as well as its color; the flower heads echo the bulbous shape of the container as well as the valet's head; and the colors of both container and flowers are subtly repeated in the fishes mounted on the wall. The alliums are pleasingly proportionate to the container, and the whole arrangement is proportionate to the tank on which it sits. It is as simple and unpretentious—and as whimsical—as its setting; everything is of a piece. Nothing is haphazard.

Historically, cut flowers have been arranged in traditional, rule-determined styles, often with intricate designs and symbolic meaning. But are simple, spontaneous little arrangements as legitimate as traditional, elaborate arrangements? Yes. Besides, decorative, simple arrangements and meaningfully expressive ones are not mutually exclusive; all arrangements are both decorative, and most arrangements are, in some sense, meaningful.

For example, a spontaneous modern arrangement, like the one shown on page 17, is wonderfully decorative, and at the same time it embodies a historical concept (the bouquet). Certainly there is nothing that makes a highly structured and symbolic ikebana design inherently better than a simple but sensitively designed nosegay. What might make one a better arrangement than another, however, is how it is

The holiday garland festooning this stairway is a modern version of a decoration dating back to ancient Greece.

Sometimes the
simplest arrange-
ments are the most
effective, as this
container with
three alliums
demonstrates.

used—its appropriateness for a particular setting or occasion. The Old Masters-inspired arrangement on page 72 is no more appropriate for the toilet tank shown here than the little container of alliums on the tank is suited to grace a Chippendale buffet. The question of appropriateness is explored further on page 67.

How Do We Use Flower Arrangements?

Making flower arrangements is a satisfying and creative way to help celebrate many of life's events. Among these events are celebration of seasons, celebration of special occasions, and enhancement of daily life.

CELEBRATION OF SEASONS

For physical comfort, privacy, and security, we set walls between ourselves and the outdoors. Yet something deep within us yearns to stay in touch with our natural surroundings. Flowers serve to bridge the gap between outdoors and indoors, bringing us closer to the seasons. Especially fortunate among us are those who have gardens that provide seasonal flowers and foliage for their arrangements. Except in winter, well-stocked gardens in most climates can provide a broader selection of plant materials than that offered by most florists.

Even a small garden in the dead of winter can provide branches, berries, cones and pods, and sometimes flowers, all of which bring indoors the freshness and subdued life of the winter garden. Holly leaves and berries in a simple vase, or a stem or so of hellebore, enliven the indoors. A forced branch flowering quince brings a foretaste of spring. At the very least, the winter garden can offer sweet-scented sprigs of evergreens and picturesque, bare branches to be supplemented by greenhouse-grown flowers from the florist.

Spring, the time of renewal of growth and blooming, is the most dramatic season in the garden. From the appearance of the first snowdrops, crocus, and other early bulbs to the blooming of lilac and early roses, which mark the transition to summer, the spring garden offers a lush display of beauty. What a luxury to bring the garden indoors with vases of scented hyacinths, apple blossoms, and daffodils. If you are a gardenless urban dweller, you can celebrate too, with a handful of tulips, an extravagant spring mix from the florist, or even a tiny bunch of fragrant violets from a sidewalk flower stall.

The amplitude of the summer garden offers the most sustained and varied display of flowers and foliage for the house. Garden roses, depending upon their type, produce a burst or a crescendo of blossoms. Lilies and jasmine come into bloom, crape myrtle makes a massive show of color, and innumerable perennials and annuals flower through much or all of the season. No matter what your style of household interior, a brimming summer garden or florist shop will tempt you to gather lavish mixed bunches as well as individual varieties of

Though they're available all year, these brightly colored gerberas in a florist display seem to proclaim summer.

Chrysanthemums
predominate in this
fall arrangement.
Candles and season-
al fruit help set the
autumnal mood.

Berries, apples, and small bromeliads added to traditional Christmas greenery and cones create an element of surprise and reinforce the color scheme.

flowers, elegant foliage such as hosta and fern, and assortments of aromatic herbs for arrangements.

Autumn brings forth such garden beauties as chrysanthemums, asters, and hardy cyclamens. In and beyond the garden, innumerable kinds of foliage smolder and blaze, berries color, and such diverse plant forms as naturally dried cow parsnip, pumpkins and gourds, and persimmons, together with foliage and berries, provide a cornucopia of materials for creative arrangements. In this season of softening light, shortening days, mists, and chilly nights, colorful arrangements both reflect the changing of the season and counteract its melancholy by displaying its bounty. Just a branch or two of coloring maple can transform a sitting area of an urban apartment into a celebration of autumn.

CELEBRATION OF SPECIAL OCCASIONS

Except for large weddings and receptions, balls, and banquets, we celebrate most of our special occasions intimately, on a smaller scale, in our homes. Cut flowers nearly always play a role in these celebrations. The informality typical of most modern life-styles often dictates that special-occasion floral designs be casual. Yet in even the most informal homes, special occasions are frequently celebrated by flower arrangements linked through their materials or design to tradition.

The Christmas season is a time for conviviality. Traditionally, cut greens have played a major role in Christmas decoration of the home, for parties as well as for the holiday season itself. The Christmas tree brings indoors the sweetness and verdure of an evergreen forest. Wreaths and garlands of pine, spruce, fir, and other evergreens, sometimes trimmed with cones, berries, and bows, extend greenery from the front door throughout the living areas of the house. Poinsettias, sometimes cut for arrangements but usually potted, are traditional sources of color. White and red florist flowers (though other colors might

An arrangement of blanket flowers, coneflowers, coreopsis, and dill lends a focal note of summer to a roof terrace.

Floating blossoms of tuberous begonia make a striking, simple centerpiece for a dinner table.

serve as well), together with evergreen branches, holly, and other greenery and trimmings, provide materials for original arrangements with traditional elements.

Other holidays call for different sorts of floral expressions. The pure-white Easter lily is available cut or potted from the florist at Easter (though not from the garden until midsummer). However, you can also convey the Easter spirit with less expensive garden flowers, especially in soft pastel tones and white, to make arrangements in nearly any style or degree of elaborateness. In sharp contrast, bright garden flowers such as red zinnias, white daisies, and blue cornflowers might ornament your Fourth of July buffet to make a holiday statement as emphatic as fireworks, watermelon, and a backyard barbecue. Tawny seasonal blossoms, pumpkins, and dried ears of Indian corn celebrate the mood of Thanksgiving as well as the autumn season and, after all, Easter, the Fourth of July, and Thanksgiving are celebrations of their seasons as much as they are celebrations of religious or patriotic occasions.

Special occasions calling for flowers in the home include, of course, not just holidays but birthday and anniversary observances, reunions with old friends and relatives, simple or elaborate gatherings of friends, and even small home weddings. For a baby shower you might make simple bouquets of white and pastel shades. A dinner party might require, aside from arrangements in sitting areas, flowers at each place setting or a low centerpiece; look at the simple solution shown and discussed on pages 88 and 89. Baskets of flowers add a rustic touch to a luncheon in the garden (a mixed basket arrangement is shown on page 17). For a child's birthday party, use bright primary colors to create a festive serving-table arrangement with a low center of gravity. Large bouquets placed at the eye level of both standing and sitting guests, but safe from elbows in crowded or heavily trafficked areas, are useful for cocktail parties and other large gatherings at home. Seasonal flowers are always appropriate, but other possibilities, such as the bold tropical flowers on page 68, might be right for your purposes. For an informal home wedding you might make some larger-than-usual arrangements (but not out of scale with the rooms) and, if the garden is used, perhaps a sumptuous, tall, rather formal arrangement on a graceful pedestal or a table.

The graciousness of a sitting room is enhanced by flowers. In the foreground are watsonias and lilies. In the background, amaryllis plants are displayed in the clear glass vase.

An arrangement with foxglove, peony, and roadside grasses and weeds adds graceful form and subtle coloration to this all-white nursery.

A vase of miniature gladioli provides color and an object for restful contemplation in this home office.

ENHANCEMENT OF EVERYDAY LIFE

Between seasons, when Christmas, Easter, and other holidays are far away, or when our lives are routine, we especially need flower arrangements in our homes for the touch of living beauty that they bestow. They may or may not reflect the season, but they always connect us physically and emotionally with the natural world, and their decorative value adds to the attractiveness of any room. Consider where in your home you might use flower arrangements to bring maximum pleasure and satisfaction.

The best places for everyday flowers are wherever you spend time in your home. Often neglected by the flower arranger is the kitchen, where flowers soften the utilitarian atmosphere. Casual flowers in simple or earthy containers are often most appropriate in a kitchen. Place arrangements in good light and in view but away from heat and heavily used surfaces. A floral touch is also welcome in a bathroom. You can work much more happily in your study or read in a sitting room with flowers at eye level, close by. Even the simplest meal for one or two can be made an occasion with candles

and a simple centerpiece. See page 12 for one effective, easy idea. Flowers can add a sense of comfort and coziness to a bedroom; just remember to position them where reaching to turn on a light will not precipitate a disaster. Do you spend part of your day in a utility room? If so, make it more habitable, maybe even pleasant or downright inviting, with bright flowers. On a well-lighted hallway table, an entryway—wherever your eye might rest—provide flowers from time to time. Remember to vary the locations in which you place arrangements from time to time so they will retain their impact.

How To Use This Book

Now that you've seen some of the many versatile ways in which flower arrangements can be used and enjoyed in your home, turn to the remaining chapters for the specifics. In the chapter that follows, you will find information on the flowers themselves: how to grow your own flowers and how to select healthy, good-quality flowers from a florist, and a lengthy chart

offering useful information about some of the best common garden and florist flowers and foliage. Then you will find a chapter with detailed information about gathering, preparing, and maintaining flowers and other arranging materials, together with instructions for up-to-date methods of preserving flowers. This chapter also discusses how to select and use equipment and containers, and describes the techniques and mechanics useful in making arrangements. A chapter on design covers the basics of form, balance, color, and other design elements, explaining what you need to know in order to create pleasing designs. This chapter will guide you in experimentation and creativity rather than prescribe rigid formulas. The final chapter displays in luxurious detail an array of widely differing arrangements, each accompanied by a discussion of how the arrangement was conceived, designed, and assembled, with ideas for appropriate settings for each design and ways that you might use it as a springboard for your own creations. The arrangements in this last chapter are intended, as is this entire book, to help you discover the unlimited possibilities in arranging flowers for your home.

An afternoon get-together in the garden becomes an occasion with the addition of flowers—lily, calla, nerine, delphinium, freesia, stephanotis, society garlic, and cosmos.

Fresh flowers just coming into bloom promise
many days of beauty in the home. Nerine is
predominant in this florist display.

FLOWERS FOR ARRANGEMENTS

The list of flowers for arrangements is endless. Growing your own flowers is satisfying and assures that you'll get what you want. Florists carry a wide assortment of flowers, including exotic varieties. Fields and roadsides can also provide many beautiful materials.

Cut flowers, with their myriad colors, scents, forms, and seasonal moods, bring into your home some of the most focused beauty of the natural world. The out-of-doors is a vast resource of decorative and interesting materials for arrangements. Besides flowers and foliage, your garden can provide you with berries, various kinds of pods and other seed structures, and bare and budded branches seasonally. Florists sell many of the common garden flowers, often carrying them much longer than the the blooming season in your own garden. Most flower shops also offer an array of exotic and tropical flowers and foliage.

Along with some pointers for growing your own flowers and buying them from a florist shop, this chapter contains a list of many of the best flowers for cutting, including information and instructions to help you select or gather them, keep them fresh, dry or preserve many of them, and make the best uses of them for your purposes. In addition, you'll find suggestions for looking beyond your garden or florist for cut flowers as well as a medley of other natural materials to augment or enhance your arrangements. Resources for flower arranging extend as far as your imagination and your creative eye allow.

Growing Your Own Flowers

Having flowers close at hand for your arrangements is just one advantage of growing flowers for cutting. Another is economy; though growing flowers requires sustained effort, expenses are minimal, usually no more than the cost of seeds, seedlings, or bulbs, plus water, fertilizer, and simple tools that you'll continue to use for many years. Their garden freshness will ensure that your cut flowers will be crisp and long lasting. One of the greatest advantages of growing your own flowers is that you can plant your favorite varieties, in colors and color combinations that you prefer. Another advantage is that you can try unusual flowers, rarely or never available from flower shops.

If you place a premium on fragrance, you can plant a galaxy of scented flowers such as gardenias, pinks, roses, narcissus, lilacs, lavender, and daphne. You can also grow your favorite kinds of foliage for arranging—perhaps southern magnolia, fern, hellebore, holly, peony, or nasturtium. If you live in a warm-winter area or have a greenhouse, you can grow tropical beauties like hibiscus, orchids, bird-of-paradise, and gloriosa lily. A greenhouse also enables you to enjoy many garden flowers that are out of season in the garden. If you're busy or have little space, even a few containers in an out-of-the-way corner of your property, on a retaining wall, or on a balcony can yield a burst of early-spring daffodils or a long season of marguerites. Whether you grow armloads of flowers for cutting or only a handful, you will take special pleasure in decorating your house with flowers that you've nurtured to maturity.

Perhaps the most valuable, if not the most obvious, advantage of growing your

A wide selection of healthy flowers in a clean, attractive setting makes this florist shop a valuable resource for arrangers.

A well-planned landscape can be decorative and still provide materials for cutting. The large flower plantings here yield more than enough flowers for arranging without appearing stripped of blooms.

own flowers is your increasing familiarity with them. You'll find that living with flowers in your garden, noticing day after day and season after season how they grow and hold their blossoms and leaves, will give you a rapport with them that lends special grace and naturalness to your arrangements.

MAKING A CUTTING GARDEN

The time, space, budget and enthusiasm that you have for gardening largely determine how many kinds of flowers you can grow, and in what quantities. Planting a large garden, carefully designed so that a backbone of evergreens together with masses of blossoms remain after you've gathered flowers, will ensure that your home landscape never looks stripped. But you should consider the obvious advantage of making a separate cutting garden whose sole purpose is to produce flowers and foliage for cutting rather than to form part of your ornamental landscape. If you have enough space, you can devote a separate area to beds, clumps, or rows of cutting flowers, laying them out like a typical

vegetable garden. Such a set-up is designed for efficiency, not decoration, makes maximum use of space, and allows for optimal sunlight and air circulation as well as ease of maintenance. Consider combining your cutting and vegetable gardens, for that matter. Even a patch of sunny ground outside your door can sustain a collection of perennial and annual herbs, which are as pleasing in vases as in cooking pots. Planters are another option if your space is limited. Grow bulbs, annuals, perennials, herbs, shrubs, or small trees in planters to provide material for your arrangements.

GARDEN CARE

No matter where or how you decide to grow flowers for cutting, bear in mind that gardening is work. However, if you enjoy plants and the outdoors, gardening can be a labor of love, and sound horticultural practices will reward you with superior flowers.

Healthy plants that receive ideal light, water, and nutrients yield cut flowers that not only look perfect but usually outlast—by days, in some cases—flowers from less vigorous plants. Too little fertilizer can

mean few and paltry flowers; so can too much fertilizer, which causes many kinds of plants to develop lush foliage instead of blossoms.

Movable containers may help you to grow first-rate flowers. Using boxes with carrying handles, small pots, or half-barrels with casters will enable you to move your plants daily or seasonally in order to take fullest advantage of sunlight, shade, and shelter from wind in a small or poorly situated garden (and to move out of view those plants stripped of flowers).

Keep in mind also that many plants bloom more vigorously for having their flowers clipped. When fading flowers are not picked off, the plant expends its energy making seed rather than new blooms. Remove flowers as soon as they begin to fade to encourage continued flower production. Further encourage their reblooming with fertilizer and regular watering.

Flowers From a Florist

If you are without a garden and can't grow any flowers for your arrangements, you are dependent largely or entirely on florists for cut flowers. Even if you have an extensive garden, you probably use florist flowers at least in winter. Advances in horticulture and transport have broadened the supply and selection of cut flowers throughout much of the country. Ginger, anthurium, and other tropical flowers and foliage are flown in from Hawaii the year around, and tulips from Dutch greenhouses are available even in the fall.

Although florists sell many of the flower varieties grown in home gardens, other florist flowers are significantly different. Just as agricultural varieties of, say, apples have been selected or bred to travel well and have a long shelf life, special florist flowers have been developed for long vase life, color that doesn't fade, and other commercially desirable qualities. Some florist flowers, such as large-blossomed chrysanthemums, are produced by particular methods of propagation, pruning, and bud thinning; special techniques yield long-stemmed blossoms in some floribunda rose varieties that in the garden might have very short stems.

When you choose a florist shop, look for one where you can get not only fresh flowers, but sound advice on the care of each type. Knowing which days shipments arrive is helpful; buy as soon as fresh flowers are set out.

The best florists buy the freshest flowers available from the most reliable sources, condition them properly, and offer them only as long as they remain fresh. Retail prices are normally higher than those in shops that sell flowers of inferior quality. See page 43 for pointers on selecting flowers at a florist shop.

Some Flowers for Arranging

The following chart lists some of the most important cut flowers for arranging. It is designed to help you select cut flowers for your immediate needs, and to guide you in selecting plants for your cutting garden. Flowering plants predominate, but also included are a number of plants important to arrangers for foliage, seed structures, and branches. A few especially attractive, widely available exotics from the florists are also included.

The list is alphabetized by botanical name because that name, unlike a plant's various common names, is universally understood. Widely used common names are included in parentheses, and a cross-reference guide, listing common names and botanical names, is given on page 39. Only the name of the genus (for example, *Acanthus*) has been given in most cases; either there is only one member of that genus that is both important to horticulture and commonly used as a cut flower, or there are several members so much alike in all pertinent respects that there is no need to name them separately. If one member of a large and diverse genus of horticulturally important plants has been singled out for inclusion here, its specific name (for example, *Salix caprea*) is given.

Plant type classifies each plant as an annual; perennial; biennial; deciduous or evergreen tree, shrub or vine; bulb (or the bulblike corm, rhizome, or tuber); or tropical plant, usually available only from florists.

Seasons refers to the seasons of usefulness to arrangers, in most cases the time of bloom. Remember that seasons differ depending on the geographical location of the garden. For example, "early spring" does not occur at the same time in Denver as it does in Savannah; there is a difference of several weeks. Also, the bloom season can vary considerably depending on the species. Whenever a cut flower is available only from a florist, or from the florist over a significantly longer period than from the garden, the period of availability from a florist is given in parentheses.

Colors indicates commonly available colors, to help you plant with color schemes in mind. Bear in mind that there are many variations within a color. For example, pink may range from pale pink to rosy pink.

Fragrance refers to blossoms, not foliage, unless otherwise indicated.

Vase life gives the approximate time a fresh stem of cut flowers can be expected to last, given proper treatment and ideal conditions (see page 45).

Uses indicates what parts of the plants are useful for arrangements (blossoms unless otherwise indicated) and whether they are useful fresh, dried, or glycerinated.

Comments includes further information that might be helpful, particularly tips on cutting, treating, conditioning, maximizing vase life, and preserving. Unless the chart indicates otherwise, assume that a plant requires standard treatment. Unless another technique is specified in the chart, "dried" means air-dried by hanging upside down (see page 49). In some cases certain standard procedures are named in the charts to emphasize their special importance for those particular plants. Information about forcing (see page 46) is included where relevant.

A cutting garden, planted in rows like a vegetable garden, supplies flowers and foliage for arrangements.

NAME	PLANT TYPE	SEASONS	COLORS
Acanthus (*Bear's breech*)	*Perennial*	*Summer*	*Mauve and white*
Acer palmatum (*Japanese maple*)	*Deciduous tree or shrub*	*Spring to fall*	*Leaves: variable by variety. Flowers: reddish*
Achillea (*Yarrow*)	*Perennial*	*Summer to early fall (spring through summer)*	*White, yellow, rose, or red*
Agapanthus (*Lily-of-the-Nile, African lily*)	*Perennial*	*Summer (late spring to summer)*	*Blue or white*
Alcea (*Hollyhock*)	*Annual or biennial*	*Summer*	*Pink, rose, purple, white, or pale yellow*
Allium (*Allium, ornamental onion*)	*Bulb*	*Late spring to summer*	*Pink, rose, red, violet, blue, white, or yellow*
Alstroemeria (*Peruvian lily*)	*Perennial*	*Summer (all year)*	*Yellow, orange, pink, red, mauve, lavender, cream, or brownish*
Anemone coronaria (*Anemone, windflower*)	*Tuberous perennial*	*Spring (winter to spring)*	*White, red, or blue, with black centers*
Anthurium (*Anthurium, flamingo flower, painted tongue*)	*Tropical perennial*	*(All year)*	*Red, orange, pink, white, or cream*
Antirrhinum (*Snapdragon*)	*Annual*	*Late spring to summer; winter and spring in mild-winter climates (all year)*	*White, pink, red, orange, or yellow*
Aquilegia (*Columbine*)	*Perennial*	*Spring to early summer*	*White, pink, cream, yellow, blue, mauve*
Aster (*Aster, Michaelmas daisy*)	*Perennial*	*Summer to fall*	*White, cream, pink, red, lavender, purple, or blue, with yellow or orange centers*
Astilbe (*False spiraea, meadowsweet*)	*Perennial*	*Summer*	*White, pink, rose, red, or deep crimson*
Calendula (*Pot marigold*)	*Annual*	*Spring and summer; winter and spring in mild-winter climates*	*Yellow, orange, apricot, or cream*
Callistephus (*China aster*)	*Annual*	*Summer to fall*	*White, pink, rose, blue, purple, violet, burgundy, or red*

Agapanthus

Alcea

FRAGRANCE	VASE LIFE	USES	COMMENTS
None	*Leaves: 2 to 6 days; flowers: to several weeks*	*Fresh or dried flowers, fresh leaves*	*Fresh: Pick mature leaves and singe or dip in boiling water, then condition. Singe or boil; see page 44. Air-dry flowers; air-dry or dessicate foliage.*
None	*6 to 12 days*	*Fresh flowers, fresh or glycerinated leaves*	*Force the tiny flowers. Cut mature foliage on hardened growth for fresh use or glycerination.*
Pleasantly bitter, herby foliage	*10 to 14 days*	*Fresh flowers; yellow varieties dry well*	*Air-dry or dry standing upright in a little water; pick when at least half the flowers are fully open. When used fresh, foliage often wilts.*
None	*5 to 7 days*	*Fresh flowers, dried seed heads*	*Use fresh, or air-dry seed heads. Fresh: Cut when one fourth of flowers are open. Drafts and temperature changes may cause flowers to drop.*
None	*5 to 8 days*	*Fresh flowers, dried seed heads*	*Fresh: Fill and plug stems, then boil ends for a minute; see page 44. Dried: Hang stems of mature seed heads to air-dry, or dry with any dessicant.*
Some sweet, a few rank	*Variable by species, to 3 weeks*	*Fresh or dried flowers; dried seed heads*	*Fresh: Pick as buds begin to open. Change water frequently if necessary because of smell. Dried: Compact types in full bloom are suitable for air-drying, as are all seed heads.*
Most scentless, a few sweet	*To 14 days*	*Fresh or dried flowers, dried seed heads*	*Fresh: Use additive to prevent foliage from wilting, or remove foliage before arranging. Dried: Air-dry seed heads.*
None	*4 to 7 days*	*Fresh or dried flowers*	*Fresh: Cut open and nearly open buds or flowers while centers are still tight. Fares poorly in floral foam. Use bleach in water. Dried: Use silica gel or borax and cornmeal, or microwave.*
None	*14 to 28 days*	*Fresh flowers and foliage*	*Select flowers whose pollen isn't yet loose. Plain, clean water is sufficient.*
In a few varieties	*6 to 12 days*	*Fresh, dried flowers*	*Fresh: Cut when bottom half of spike is flowering. Stems turn and reach toward light. Dried: Use silica gel.*
Delicate or none	*2 to 5 days*	*Fresh flowers, dried seed heads*	*Fresh: Pick before fully opened. Add bleach to water. Dried: Air-dry seed heads.*
None	*7 to 10 days*	*Fresh flowers*	*Remove every leaf below water level. Scrape, split, and boil stem ends. Use sugar solution. If possible, recut stems daily.*
None	*5 to 7 days*	*Fresh flowers, dried seed heads*	*Fresh: Split stem ends. Dried: Pick and air-dry when all flowers are open; air-dry seed heads.*
Lightly pungent flowers and foliage	*6 to 14 days*	*Fresh flowers*	*Be sure to remove all foliage below water level. Cut when outer two thirds of petals are developed.*
None	*8 to 14 days*	*Fresh flowers*	*Be sure to remove all foliage below water level.*

NAME	PLANT TYPE	SEASONS	COLORS
Calluna (Scotch heather)	Evergreen shrub	Midsummer to fall	White, pink, lavender, or purple
Camellia (Camellia)	Evergreen shrub	Fall to midspring	White, pink, rose, or red
Campanula (Bellflower)	Annual or perennial	Spring to fall	Blue, lavender-blue, white, purple, or pink
Centaurea cyanus (Cornflower, bachelor's button)	Annual	Summer (spring to summer)	Light and dark blue, white, pink, rose, or burgundy
Chaenomeles (Flowering quince)	Deciduous shrub	Winter to early spring	Red, pink, coral, or white
Chrysanthemum frutescens (Marguerite)	Perennial	Summer (all year)	Yellow or white with golden center
C. maximum (Shasta daisy)	Perennial	Summer	White, usually with golden center
C. × morifolium (Florist's chrysanthemum)	Perennial	Late summer to fall (all year)	White, yellow, bronze, pink, red, lavender, purple, or bicolored
Clematis (Clematis)	Deciduous or evergreen vine	Spring to summer	White, pink, blue, purple, or mauve
Consolida (Larkspur, annual delphinium)	Annual	Spring to midsummer	White, blue, pink, red, lilac, salmon, or purple
Convallaria (Lily-of-the-valley)	Perennial	Late spring to early summer (all year)	White, sometimes pink
Cordyline terminalis (Ti)	Tropical shrub	(All year)	Green or red-green
Coreopsis (Coreopsis)	Annual or perennial	Summer	Yellow, gold, mahogany, or bicolored
Cornus (Dogwood)	Deciduous tree	Spring	White or pink
Cosmos (Cosmos)	Annual	Summer to fall	White, pink, rose, or orange-red
Crataegus (Hawthorn)	Deciduous tree	Late spring	White, pink, or scarlet

Centaurea cyanus 'Blue Boy'

Convallaria

Cosmos

FRAGRANCE	VASE LIFE	USES	COMMENTS
None	*7 to 10 days or longer*	*Fresh or dried flowers; glycerinated foliage and flowers*	*Fresh: Gather young blooms and split the stems. Dried: Stand stems of young blooms upright in a little water; see page 49. Hair spray helps hold fresh or dried flowers. Glycerinated foliage and flowers: Hammer stems.*
A few varieties are sweet	*3 to 6 days*	*Fresh flowers and leaves; glycerinated leaves*	*Fresh: Cut and split short stems when flowers are just opening. Sometimes used in corsages, though flowers bruise and shatter easily. If you float the flowers, keep water off petals and centers.*
None	*7 to 14 days*	*Fresh flowers*	*Split stems of woody types and sear or boil for a minute.*
None	*5 to 7 days*	*Fresh or dried flowers*	*Cut fully open but unfaded flowers. Dry flower heads with a dessicant, or air-dry.*
None	*6 to 10 days*	*Fresh flowers*	*A classic for forcing; see page 46.*
Slight	*3 to 6 days*	*Fresh flowers*	*Be sure to remove every leaf below water level.*
Slight	*3 to 6 days*	*Fresh flowers*	*Be sure to remove every leaf below water level.*
Herby foliage and flowers	*1 to 2 weeks*	*Fresh or dried flowers*	*Fresh: See page 44 for treatment. Be sure to remove all foliage below water level, but not upper foliage unless it is damaged or begins to yellow. Dried: Use microwave.*
Evergreen species very fragrant	*2 to 3 days*	*Fresh flowers, dried seed heads*	*Fresh: Boil or singe stem ends. Dried: See page 48 for how to preserve seed heads.*
None	*6 to 10 days*	*Fresh or dried flowers, dried seed heads*	*Fresh: Cut when bottom third of flowers are open. Dried: Cut when half or more of flowers are newly opened; air-dry or use borax and cornmeal. Air-dry seed heads.*
Strong, sweet	*3 to 6 days*	*Fresh flowers and foliage, dried flowers, glycerinated leaves*	*Fresh: Cut or buy when top buds are closed but showing color. Dried: Use any dessicant. Glycerinated leaves: Submerge entirely in half water, half glycerine for about a week.*
None	*1 to 2 weeks*	*Fresh or glycerinated leaves*	*Useful for creating bold, tropical effect.*
None or slight	*1 to 2 weeks*	*Fresh flowers*	*Cut fully opened flowers with tight centers.*
None or slight	*8 to 10 days*	*Fresh flowers, berries, foliage, dried flowers*	*Fresh: Cut when "petals" (actually bracts) have developed but before pollen appears. Split stems. Or force when buds begin to enlarge. Dried flowers: Use microwave.*
None	*5 to 7 days*	*Fresh or dried flowers*	*Fresh: Select flowers whose pollen hasn't yet developed. Dried: Use borax or silica gel crystals.*
Scentless or slightly rank. English Hawthorn is sweet	*3 to 7 days*	*Fresh flowers, fresh or air-dried berries*	*Dry berries with stems upright. To force flowers, cut 4 to 6 weeks before blooming time.*

Dahlia

Digitalis

Echinops

NAME	PLANT TYPE	SEASONS	COLORS
Dahlia (*Dahlia*)	*Tuberous perennial*	*Midsummer to fall*	*All colors but green and blue*
Daphne (*Daphne*)	*Evergreen or deciduous shrub*	*Late winter to spring*	*Rose pink to deep red*
Delphinium (*Delphinium*)	*Perennial*	*Late spring to early fall*	*Blue, red, purple, lavender, yellow, or white*
Dianthus barbatus (*Sweet William*)	*Biennial*	*Summer*	*Purple, red, pink, rose, white, mauve, or bicolored*
D. caryophyllus (*Carnation*)	*Perennial*	*Summer (all year)*	*Red, white, pink, yellow, orange, apricot, or bicolored*
D. deltoides *and other species* (*Pinks*)	*Perennial, biennial, or annual*	*Spring to summer*	*White, pink, rose, mauve, or red*
Digitalis (*Foxglove*)	*Biennial or perennial*	*Late spring to early summer*	*White, cream, pink, rose, red, or purple*
Echinops (*Globe thistle*)	*Perennial*	*Summer (midspring to summer)*	*Blue, sometimes white*
Eremurus (*Foxtail lily, desert candle*)	*Perennial*	*Early summer*	*White, pink, peach, or yellow*
Erica (*Heath*)	*Evergreen shrub*	*All year, depending on species*	*White, pink, rose, red, purple, or lilac*
Eryngium (*Sea holly*)	*Perennial*	*Summer*	*Silvery blue or amethyst*
Eucalyptus pulverulenta *and other species* (*Eucalyptus*)	*Evergreen tree*	*(All year)*	*Gray to green*
Euphorbia pulcherrima (*Poinsettia*)	*Tropical shrub*	*(Early winter)*	*Red, white, or pink*
Fern — *many genera and species* (*Fern*)	*Perennial foliage plant*	*All year, depending on species (all year)*	*Varies from light to dark green*
Forsythia (*Forsythia*)	*Deciduous shrub*	*Late winter to early spring*	*Yellow*
Freesia (*Freesia*)	*Corm*	*Early spring (all year)*	*Yellow, white, cream, red, pink, purple, lavender, or blue*

FRAGRANCE	VASE LIFE	USES	COMMENTS
None	*5 to 7 days*	*Fresh or dried flowers*	*Fresh: Cut as soon as flowers have fully opened. Remove all leaves below water level. Dried: Dry in sand. Pompom types dry best.*
Heavy, sweet	*3 to 6 days*	*Fresh flowers*	*Cut judiciously from these slow-growing shrubs.*
None	*5 to 8 days*	*Fresh or dried flowers, dried seed heads*	*Fresh: For preparation, see page 44. Dried: Air-dry*
Lightly clove-scented	*7 to 12 days*	*Fresh flowers*	*Cut stems at a slant above joints and split larger stems.*
Very spicy	*7 to 12 days*	*Fresh or dried flowers*	*Fresh: Needs same treatment as **D. barbatus**. Dried: Use microwave.*
Some very spicy	*5 to 12 days*	*Fresh flowers*	*Be sure to cut stems under water, and recut periodically to extend vase life.*
None	*5 to 10 days*	*Fresh or glycerinated flowers, dried seed heads*	*Fresh: Cut when one fourth to one half of flowers are open, and place immediately in 100° F water. Fill and plug hollow stems as described on page 44. Air-dry seed heads.*
Most are scentless	*5 to 7 days*	*Fresh or dried flowers*	*Fresh: Split stems. Dried: Pick when globes are blue but before tubes are visible. Air-dry.*
A few are sweetly scented	*4 to 7 days*	*Fresh flowers*	*Cut when about half of flowers on stalk are open.*
Some varieties are sweet	*7 to 10 days*	*Fresh or dried flowers and foliage*	*Same treatment as for **Calluna**.*
None	*—*	*Dried flowers*	*Air-dry or use dessicant.*
Foliage of many species very fragrant	*To several weeks*	*Fresh foliage, glycerinated and dried foliage, and dried seed capsules*	*Fresh foliage: Split stems. Glycerinated foliage: Split stems before treating. Hang to air-dry.*
None	*4 to 5 days*	*Fresh flowers*	*For treatment, see page 44. Consider disguising its pot to make a poinsettia plant part of a large arrangement.*
None	*Variable, to 14 days*	*Fresh, dried, and glycerinated foliage*	*Fresh: Submerge garden types in cold water for 2 to 8 hours (longer for less delicate types). Dried: Air-dry sturdier types.*
None	*7 to 14 days*	*Fresh flowers*	*Cut branches just as they start to flower. Cut several weeks earlier to force.*
Faint to strong, sweet	*5 to 12 days*	*Fresh or dried flowers*	*Fresh: Cut just when first 3 or 4 flowers on each spike are open. Additive containing sugar enables all buds to open. Dried: Use silica gel.*

Gladiolus

NAME	PLANT TYPE	SEASONS	COLORS
Fritillaria imperialis (*Crown imperial*)	*Bulb*	*Spring*	*Red, orange, or yellow*
Fuchsia (*Fuchsia*)	*Deciduous shrub*	*Summer*	*Red, pink, rose, salmon, coral, purple, cream, white, or bicolored*
Gaillardia (*Blanket flower*)	*Perennial*	*Summer to fall*	*Red, yellow, orange, or maroon; often banded*
Gardenia (*Gardenia, Cape jasmine*)	*Evergreen shrub*	*Summer (all year)*	*White, aging to ivory*
Gerbera (*Gerbera, Transvaal daisy*)	*Perennial*	*Summer (all year)*	*Yellow, cream, orange, coral, pink, or red*
Geum (*Geum*)	*Perennial*	*Late spring to late summer*	*Yellow, orange, or red*
Gladiolus (*Gladiolus*)	*Corm*	*Spring to summer (all year)*	*All colors but true blue, some bicolors*
Gloriosa (*Gloriosa lily, glory lily*)	*Tuberous vine*	*Spring to summer (all year)*	*Red bordered by yellow*
Gomphrena (*Globe amaranth*)	*Annual*	*Midsummer to early fall*	*Rose, red, orange, purple, or white*
Gypsophila (*Baby's breath*)	*Annual, perennial*	*Summer (all year)*	*White or pink*
Hamamelis (*Witch hazel*)	*Deciduous shrub*	*Winter*	*Golden yellow, red, or copper*
Hedera helix (*English ivy*)	*Evergreen vine*	*All year*	*Green or variegated*
Helianthus (*Sunflower*)	*Annual*	*Late summer*	*Yellow or yellow-copper bicolored*
Helichrysum (*Strawflower*)	*Annual*	*Summer to early fall*	*Pink, red, orange, yellow, or white*
Heliconia (*Lobster claw*)	*Tropical perennial*	*(All year)*	*Red and yellow*
Helleborus (*Hellebore*)	*Evergreen perennial*	*Fall to spring, depending on species*	*White, pink, purple, or green*
Hemerocallis (*Daylily*)	*Tuberous perennial*	*Summer*	*Cream, yellow, orange, mahogany, pink, apricot, or bicolored*

Hemerocallis 'New Yorker'

FRAGRANCE	VASE LIFE	USES	COMMENTS
Slight, rank	4 to 7 days	Fresh flowers	Cut when more than half of flowers in cluster are open.
None	5 to 7 days	Fresh flowers	Split stems.
None	6 to 10 days	Fresh flowers	Cut when centers are still tight. Split stems and remove leaves below water level. Condition with additive containing sugar.
Strong, very sweet	2 to 5 days	Fresh flowers with foliage	Cut as soon as blooms are fully open. Petals bruise easily when handled. Condition in cold water. Flowers without foliage can be floated.
None	Variable, to 3 weeks	Fresh flowers	Cut when 2 rows of pollen appear. Split stems. Condition and keep in solution containing sugar. Stems turn and reach toward light. Handle with care; top-heavy flowers can snap stems.
None	4 to 7 days	Fresh flowers	Cut when flowers are nearly open.
None	7 to 14 days	Fresh flowers	Cut after 3 or 4 flowers open on the spike. Use additive containing sugar. Tips bend upward when stems are laid horizontally.
None	4 to 8 days	Fresh flowers and foliage	Buy stems of flowers whose petals haven't yet turned all the way back. Split stems.
None	5 to 7 days	Fresh or dried flowers	Fresh: Cut when flowers are nearly open. Split stems. Dried: Cut when flowers are fully globe shaped. Remove foliage and air-dry flowers.
None	5 to 7 days	Fresh or dried flowers	Fresh: Cut when about half of flowers are open. Dried: Cut just when in full bloom. Hang or dry upright in shallow water; see page 49
Sweet	5 to 7 days	Fresh flowers	Branches cut in early winter force in about a week.
None	To several weeks	Fresh or glycerinated foliage	To preserve, submerge in solution of half glycerine, half water.
Slightly aromatic	6 to 10 days	Fresh flowers, dried seed heads	Fresh: Cut just when petals turn back and centers are still tight. If necessary, reinforce stems with heavy wire or wire and reeds or sticks. Dried seed heads: Leave them on the plant until dry.
None	7 to 14 days	Fresh or dried flowers	Fresh: Stems rot once flowers begin to dry out. Dried: Pick when just starting to open. Remove leaves and air-dry flowers.
None	7 to 14 days	Fresh flowers	Select stems with a few unopened buds.
None	To several weeks	Fresh or dried flowers; glycerinated foliage	Fresh: Singe or scald stem ends. Dried: Use any dessicant.
Some yellow varieties very sweet	To 14 days	Fresh flowers and foliage	Individual blossoms open during the day, wither at night, are replaced by opening buds on successive days. To have open flowers at night, refrigerate during the day.

NAME	PLANT TYPE	SEASONS	COLORS
Heuchera sanguinea *(Coral bells)*	*Perennial*	*Midspring to late summer*	*Pink, red, coral, and white*
Hibiscus rosa-sinensis *(Hibiscus)*	*Tropical evergreen shrub*	*Summer*	*White, yellow, red, rose, pink, apricot, or coral*
Hippeastrum *(Amaryllis)*	*Bulb*	*(Fall to spring)*	*White, red, pink, salmon, orange, or bicolored*
Hosta *(Hosta, plantain lily)*	*Perennial*	*Flowers summer, leaves spring to summer*	*White to lilac. Leaves various greens, some species variegated*
Hyacinthus *(Hyacinth)*	*Bulb*	*Late winter to spring*	*White, cream, red, rose, pink, blue, or purple*
Hydrangea *(Hydrangea)*	*Deciduous shrub*	*Summer*	*White, red, pink, or blue*
Iberis *(Candytuft)*	*Annual or perennial*	*Late spring to midsummer*	*White, lavender, pink, mauve, or red*
Ilex *(Holly)*	*Evergreen shrub or tree*	*All year (winter)*	*Glossy green*
Iris, *bearded (Iris)*	*Rhizome*	*Late spring to early summer*	*All but green*
Iris, *Dutch, English, and Spanish (Iris)*	*Bulb*	*Spring (all year)*	*White, orange, yellow, blue, purple, mauve, or bicolored*
Kniphofia *(Red-hot poker, torch lily)*	*Perennial*	*Spring to early fall*	*Coral, yellow, cream, or bicolored*
Lathyrus *(Sweet pea)*	*Annual*	*Spring to summer*	*White, cream, pink, purple, red, or orange*
Lavandula *(Lavender)*	*Evergreen shrub*	*Summer*	*Lavender or purple*
Liatris *(Blazing star, gayfeather)*	*Perennial*	*Summer (all year)*	*Rose-purple*
Lilium *(Lily)*	*Bulb*	*Summer (all year)*	*White, yellow, pink, rose, red, orange, and bicolored*
Limonium *(Statice, sea lavender)*	*Perennial or annual*	*Summer (all year)*	*Lavender, blue, white, yellow, rose, or bicolored*

Ilex

Lilium

Limonium

FRAGRANCE	VASE LIFE	USES	COMMENTS
None	*5 to 8 days*	*Fresh flowers*	*Cut when about half the flowers on the stem are open.*
None	*1 to 3 days*	*Fresh flowers*	*Split stems.*
None	*5 to 7 days*	*Fresh flowers*	*Fill stems with water and plug them; see page 44. You can also make potted amaryllis the center of an arrangement.*
Most are scentless	*5 to 7 days*	*Fresh flowers and foliage, dried foliage*	*Fresh: Cut when 3 or 4 flowers have opened. Split stems and condition in cold water nearly up to blossoms. Dried foliage: Air-dry in dark place.*
Strong, sweet	*2 to 6 days*	*Fresh flowers*	*Gather when about half the flowers are open, and keep separate from other flowers for an hour after picking, until sap has drained. If wilting occurs, dip stems in boiling water for a minute.*
None	*6 to 12 days*	*Fresh or dried flowers*	*Fresh: Treat like other woody-stemmed flowers; see page 44. Boil or sear stem ends. Submerge wilted flower heads until they revive. Dried: Pick when flowers are papery; air-dry or stand upright in shallow water; see page 49.*
Sweet	*5 to 7 days*	*Fresh flowers, dried seed heads*	*Cut when half the flowers are open. Split any hard stems. Remove foliage below water level.*
None	*To several weeks*	*Fresh foliage and berries, glycer-inated foliage*	*Treat like other woody-stemmed plants; see page 44.*
Rich	*2 to 5 days*	*Fresh flowers*	*Cut when first bud is nearly open. Use additive containing sugar.*
Sweet	*3 to 6 days*	*Fresh or dried flowers*	*Fresh: Same as bearded **Iris**, above. Dried: Select young blossoms and use microwave.*
None	*6 to 8 days*	*Fresh flowers*	*Cut when less than half of flowers have opened. Split stems.*
Sweet	*6 to 8 days*	*Fresh flowers*	*Cut before tips of clusters are in flower. Condition in no more than 2 inches of water. Use an additive containing sugar. Avoid wetting flowers.*
Fragrant flowers and leaves	*7 to 14 days*	*Fresh flowers and leaves, dried flowers*	*Fresh: Cut when half of flowers are open. Split stems. Dried: Cut when most flowers are open. Air-dry.*
Little or none	*6 to 10 days*	*Fresh or dried flowers*	*Fresh: Treat like other woody-stemmed flowers; see page 44. Dried: Air-dry when most flowers toward top of spike are open.*
Some are very fragrant	*6 to 8 days*	*Fresh flowers*	*Split stems and remove all leaves below water level. Pollen can damage furniture, so consider removing anthers.*
None	*Will last indefinitely*	*Fresh or dried flowers*	*Fresh and dried: Cut when all flowers have opened, in dry weather. Air-dry.*

NAME	PLANT TYPE	SEASONS	COLORS
Lunaria (Money plant, honesty)	Biennial	Late spring to early summer	White, rose, lavender, or purple
Lupinus (Lupine)	Annual or perennial	Late spring to early summer	Blue, white, red, rose, yellow, or bicolored
Magnolia grandiflora (Southern magnolia)	Evergreen tree	Summer	White
M. soulangiana and other deciduous types (Saucer magnolia and others)	Deciduous tree	Early to mid spring	White, pink, or purplish
Malus (Apple and crabapple)	Deciduous tree	Spring	White, pink, rose, or red, often with darker buds
Matthiola (Stock)	Annual	Spring and summer; fall to spring in mild-winter areas	White, pink, lavender, purple, red, or pale yellow
Moluccella (Bells of Ireland)	Annual	Late summer	Light green
Muscari (Grape hyacinth)	Bulb	Early spring (fall to late spring)	Blue
Myosotis (Forget-me-not)	Annual, biennial, or perennial	Early spring to early summer	Blue, sometimes pink or white
Narcissus (Daffodil and narcissus)	Bulb	Fall to spring	Yellow, white, cream, orange, red, or bicolored
Nerine (Nerine, Guernsey lily)	Bulb	Late summer to fall (all year)	White, scarlet, rose-pink, orange-red, or mauve
Nicotiana (Flowering tobacco)	Annual	Summer	White, rose, mauve, crimson, or green
Orchid — various genera (Orchid)	Tropical perennial	(All year)	All but true blue
Ornithogalum (Star-of-Bethlehem, chincherinchee)	Bulb	Spring to early summer (all year)	White or greenish white
Paeonia (Peony)	Perennial or deciduous shrub	Spring	White, pink, rose, red, mauve, cream, or yellow

Narcissus

Paeonia

FRAGRANCE	VASE LIFE	USES	COMMENTS
None	*5 to 7 days*	*Fresh flowers, dried seed pods*	*Fresh: Cut when half of flowers open. Dried: Cut when pods have begun to dry and fade. Air-dry. Gently remove the covering from each pod.*
Some are sweet or peppery	*5 to 7 days*	*Fresh flowers*	*Cut when nearly half of flowers are open. Remove foliage below water level and split stems, then fill and plug; see page 44.*
Rich	*1 to 2 days*	*Fresh flowers and foliage, glycerinated foliage*	*Fresh: Cut as petals of buds begin to loosen. Treat like other woody-stemmed flowers; see page 44. Submerge bud briefly, being careful not to bruise it. Glycerinated: For foliage only, use a tablespoon of glycerine per quart of water to condition.*
Sweet	*2 to 4 days*	*Fresh flowers*	*Cut when buds are about to open and treat like other woody-stemmed plants (page 44), or force when dormant buds begin to swell.*
Many varieties are sweet	*7 to 10 days*	*Fresh flowers*	*Cut when first blossoms have opened. Split stems and treat like other woody-stemmed plants; see page 44. To force, cut from midwinter to early spring.*
Spicy	*8 to 12 days*	*Fresh flowers*	*Use flowers from robust plants grown in full sun. Cut when nearly half of buds are open. Split stems deeply, remove every leaf below water level, and condition in chilled water containing sugar.*
Slight or none	*7 to 14 days*	*Fresh, dried, and glycerinated flowers*	*Dried: Pick when flowers (actually calyxes) have begun to dry. Stand upright in shallow water; see page 49. To glycerinate, submerge entire flower stem.*
Faint to strong spiciness	*3 to 7 days*	*Fresh or dried flowers, dried seed pods*	*Fresh: Split stems and condition in cold water. Dried flowers: Use silica gel. Dried seed pods: Pick after they have split open.*
Some are scented during evening hours	*3 to 5 days*	*Fresh flowers*	*If stems wilt, dip ends into boiling water before conditioning in cold water.*
Slight to very sweet	*4 to 6 days*	*Fresh or dried flowers*	*Fresh: Cut just as bud begins to open. See page 42 for special treatment. Split stems and condition in cold water above splits. Keep in water containing sugar. Dried: Use silica gel.*
None	*6 to 8 days*	*Fresh flowers*	*Cut when clusters are about half open. Split stems.*
Most are very sweet	*5 to 7 days*	*Fresh flowers*	*Flowers of some varieties close during the day. Cut when 2 or 3 flowers in a cluster have opened. Split woodier stems.*
Some are fragrant	*Variable but generally long, to 3 weeks*	*Fresh or dried flowers*	*Fresh: Flowers aren't cut until fully developed. All last longest in cool, moderately humid spot. Avoid wetting blossoms. Dried: Fresh blossoms of some species dry well with microwave.*
Some species are fragrant	*6 to 8 days*	*Fresh or dried flowers*	*Fresh: Flowers close at night. Cut above white base of stem. Dried: Use borax or borax and cornmeal.*
Sweet	*7 to 10 days*	*Fresh or dried flowers; glycerinated leaves*	*Fresh: Cut when flowers are open enough to show their color. Split stems and condition in cold water. In warm weather submerge flowers and stems for 1 or 2 hours. Arrange in sugar solution. Dried: Air-dry, dessicate in sand, or use microwave.*

NAME	PLANT TYPE	SEASONS	COLORS
Papaver nudicaule *(Iceland poppy)*	*Perennial; annual in warm-winter climates*	*Late spring to early fall; winter to spring in mild-winter climates*	*White, cream, yellow, orange, red, or rose*
P. orientale *(Oriental poppy)*	*Perennial*	*Late spring to early summer*	*White, red, orange, or pink*
Pelargonium *(Geranium)*	*Perennial or annual*	*Spring to fall*	*Scarlet, white, pink, lilac, salmon, or bicolored*
Penstemon *(Penstemon)*	*Perennial*	*Spring to summer*	*White, red, pink, blue, salmon, purple, or yellow*
Philadelphus *(Mock orange)*	*Deciduous shrub*	*Late spring to early summer*	*White*
Phlox *(Phlox)*	*Annual or perennial*	*Late spring to summer (late spring to fall)*	*White, cream, pink, coral, red, lavender, or purple*
Polianthes *(Tuberose)*	*Tuber*	*Summer to fall (all year)*	*White*
Protea *(Protea)*	*Evergreen shrub*	*(All year)*	*White, buff, rose, pink, crimson, salmon, white, or bicolored*
Prunus *(Plum, flowering plum, cherry, flowering cherry, and peach)*	*Deciduous tree*	*Early spring (midwinter to spring)*	*White, pink, or reddish*
Ranunculus *(Persian ranunculus)*	*Tuber*	*Late spring to early summer (winter to summer)*	*White, cream, yellow, orange, red, or pink*
Rhododendron *(Rhododendron)*	*Evergreen shrub*	*Spring to early summer*	*White, pink, rose, red, purple, or lavender*
Rosa *(Rose)*	*Deciduous shrub and climbing shrub*	*Spring to fall (all year)*	*All but blue and purple, including bi- and multicolors*
Rudbeckia *(Coneflower)*	*Annual, biennial, or perennial*	*Summer to fall*	*Yellow, reddish-brown, or bicolored, some with dark centers*
Salix caprea *(Pussy willow)*	*Deciduous shrub or tree*	*Late winter to early spring*	*Pinkish gray*
S. matsudana 'Tortuosa' (Corkscrew willow)	*Deciduous tree*	*All year*	*—*

Hybrid tea rose 'Pristine'

Salix caprea

FRAGRANCE	VASE LIFE	USES	COMMENTS
None	*2 to 5 days*	*Fresh flowers, dried seed heads*	*Fresh: Pick when buds begin to loosen. Singe stem ends or dip into boiling water, then condition in cold water and arrange in water containing sugar. Dried: Pick seed heads green and dry upright.*
None	*4 to 5 days*	*Fresh flowers, dried seed heads*	*Same treatment as for* **P. nudicaule.**
Little, but scented types have very fragrant leaves	*5 to 7 days*	*Fresh flowers*	*Cut clusters that have just started to flower. Remove all leaves below water level. Handle gently.*
None	*6 to 8 days*	*Fresh flowers*	*Cut when fewer than half of flowers have opened. Split stems.*
Very sweet	*6 to 9 days*	*Fresh flowers*	*Cut when fewer than half of flowers have opened, and remove some foliage. Treat like other woody-stemmed plants; see page 44. Force in early spring.*
Some are sweet	*Variable, to 10 days*	*Fresh flowers*	*Cut above a stem joint before half of flowers are open, and condition in cold water for at least 8 hours.*
Powerfully sweet	*7 to 14 days*	*Fresh flowers*	*Cut before lowest flowers begin to wither. Split stems. Condition in cold water up to flower heads. Recutting stems prolongs life.*
None	*To several weeks*	*Fresh or dried flowers*	*Fresh: Split stems and dip in boiling water, then condition in warm water. Dried: Stand upright in shallow water; see page 49.*
Most are sweet	*7 to 14 days*	*Fresh flowers*	*Cut varieties with single blossoms when first flowers on the branches have opened, and varieties with double blossoms when more than half have opened. Split stems and treat like other woody-stemmed plants; see page 44. Force when buds begin to swell in late winter or early spring.*
None	*7 to 14 days*	*Fresh flowers*	*Cut before fully open. Split stems and dip ends in boiling water.*
Light or none	*7 to 10 days*	*Fresh flowers and foliage; glycerinated foliage*	*Cut when fewer than half the flowers of a cluster have opened. Split stems, and submerge flowers and leaves for 2 hours in cool water. Force in late winter. Glycerination: In winter, first submerge foliage in water for a day.*
Many are fragrant to extremely fragrant	*Quite variable, most 3 to 7 days*	*Fresh or dried flowers, fresh seed structures*	*Fresh: Cut with sharp shears when outer petals begin to unfold or, for variety, cut at all stages but fully open. Remove only thorns and leaves below water level. When arranging in water, immerse stems to two thirds of their length. If possible, change water daily, always using new additive. Cut stems of florist roses and recondition; if wilted, stems should be split and plunged into 100° F water. Dried: Dry loose buds or half-opened flowers in sand for about 4 days (for large-flowered types, remove and wire blossoms before drying), or air-dry quickly or use microwave.*
None	*7 to 14 days*	*Fresh or dried flowers*	*Cut fresh, tight-centered flowers, split stems, immerse stems and foliage in cool water with sugar to condition. Later, remove any foliage that wilts.*
None	*2 to 3 weeks*	*Fresh catkins*	*Cut and split stems when fewer than half of catkins have developed. Force when catkins, still encased, begin to swell.*
None	*Will keep indefinitely*	*Bare branches, fresh or dried*	*Strip foliage if branches are in leaf.*

NAME	PLANT TYPE	SEASONS	COLORS
Scabiosa (Pincushion flower)	Annual or perennial	Midsummer to early fall	Blue, lavender, white, pink, purple, or maroon
Schizanthus (Poor man's orchid, butterfly flower)	Annual	Summer; winter to spring in mild-winter climates	White, lavender, purple, rose, and pink, heavily shaded and marked
Scilla (Bluebell, squill)	Bulb	Late winter to late spring	Blue, bluish purple, white, pink, or blue-violet
Spiraea (Spiraea)	Deciduous shrub	Late spring to early fall	White, pink, or rose red
Stephanotis (Madagascar jasmine)	Evergreen tropical vine	(All year)	White
Stokesia (Stokes' aster)	Perennial	Summer to early fall	White, blue, or purplish
Strelitzia (Bird-of-paradise)	Tropical perennial	(All year)	Orange-blue-white
Syringa (Lilac)	Deciduous shrub	Spring (late fall to spring)	White, pink, lilac, blue, rose-lavender, reddish purple, or red
Tagetes (Marigold)	Annual	Summer to fall	Yellow, gold, orange, red, cream, and bicolored
Tropaeolum (Nasturtium)	Annual	Summer	Orange, gold, red, maroon, or cream
Tulipa (Tulip)	Bulb	Spring (fall to spring)	All but true blue; some bicolors
Viola odorata (Sweet violet)	Perennial	Late winter to spring	Blue, purple, white, or bluish rose
V. × wittrockiana (Pansy)	Annual	Spring to fall; fall to spring in mild-winter climates	White, blue, purple, mahogany, rose, apricot, yellow, or bicolored
Watsonia (Watsonia)	Corm	Spring to summer	White, pink, rose, red, or deep salmon
Wisteria (Wisteria)	Deciduous woody vine	Mid- to late spring	White, blue-violet, sometimes pink or purple
Zantedeschia (Calla lily)	Rhizome	Summer (spring to summer)	White
Zinnia (Zinnia)	Annual	Summer	All but blue

Tagetes 'Gold Star'

Zinnia 'Fruitbowl Mix'

FRAGRANCE	VASE LIFE	USES	COMMENTS
Soft, slight	4 to 9 days	Fresh flowers, dried seed heads	Fresh: Cut when open or nearly open. Split stems, remove leaves, and condition in cold water. Dried: Gather when petals have fallen; air-dry.
None	4 to 7 days	Fresh flowers	Cut when clusters are at least half open. Split stems and singe or dip in boiling water.
Sweet	4 to 8 days	Fresh flowers	Plunge stems into boiling water before conditioning.
Light or none	5 to 8 days	Fresh flowers	Cut when less than half of flowers on branch are open. Split stems and treat like other woody-stemmed plants; see page 44. Or force when buds begin to swell.
Heavy, sweet	3 to 5 days	Fresh flowers	Sear stem ends or dip in boiling water, then condition in cold water. Avoid bruising flowers. Cover and refrigerate if used for wedding bouquet or corsage—do not store in a refrigerator with fresh fruit.
None	6 to 10 days	Fresh or dried flowers	Fresh: Remove foliage below water level. Split stems. If wilting occurs, place stems in 100° F water. Condition in sugar solution (1 teaspoon sugar per quart of water). Dried: Use silica gel.
None	7 to 12 days	Fresh or dried flowers	Fresh: Use additive in vase and change water every 3 days. Dried: Air-dry standing in a little water that you allow to evaporate, or use a dessicant.
Strong and sweet	5 to 7 days	Fresh flowers	Cut when less than half the blooms in cluster are open. Remove foliage. Treat like a woody-stemmed plant (page 44). Condition in cold water. Force by placing in 110° F water for several days, then in cool water.
Foliage of most is strong	7 to 14 days	Fresh or dried flowers	Fresh: Cut while centers are still tight and firm. Remove foliage. Dried: Use sand or silica gel to dry blossoms of African marigold, or use microwave.
Peppery	3 to 5 days (foliage to 2 weeks)	Fresh flowers and leaves	Split stems. Condition leaves in 100° F water, flowers in cool water. Flowers will turn toward light source.
Little or none	6 to 8 days	Fresh or dried flowers	Fresh: Cut when buds are nearly ready to open. Remove white stem base, then split stems. Wrap bunch in a rather tight cylinder of cellophane or paper to prevent heads from drooping and stems from bending during conditioning. Blossoms reach toward light source and stems continue to grow. Dried: Select young blossoms and use microwave.
Delicate, sweet	4 to 7 days	Fresh flowers	Pick when open. Immerse stems and blossoms in cold water for 1 to 2 hours. In vase, spray occasionally to keep blossoms moist.
Slight	3 to 6 days	Fresh or dried flowers	Fresh: Pick just when fully open. Dried: Use microwave.
Most are scentless	5 to 8 days	Fresh flowers	Choose stems with no more than half of buds opened.
Light to heavy	5 to 7 days	Fresh flowers	Pick when the first flowers of the cluster are open. Split stems. Spray flowers occasionally to keep from drying out. Force 4 to 6 weeks before natural bloom time.
None	5 to 7 days	Fresh flowers and foliage	Gather well-developed buds or unfurled flowers. Immerse leaves for several hours.
None	7 to 14 days	Fresh or dried flowers	Fresh: Choose open flowers with tight centers. Remove most leaves. Place stems in boiling water for a minute before conditioning. Reinforce heavy heads, which tend to break stems, with wires or toothpicks through blossoms. Dried: Wire flower heads, then dry in sand, silica gel, or borax.

Fennel is one of the many roadside weeds that are such valuable resources for the creative arranger.

Other Materials for Arrangements

Your options for arranging extend beyond flowers from your garden or a florist. Many special materials are yours for the taking if you ramble along roadsides, into fields, along beaches, or just through vacant lots. The myriad forms and subtle colors of wild grasses and weeds rival those of their cultivated cousins. Fresh or naturally dried Queen Anne's lace and fennel have few equals in the garden for strong but airy architectural form. The wiry, arching, or erect stems of innumerable wild grasses

create soft or bold effects in arrangements. Be aware, however, that many wildflower populations are dwindling toward extinction, so be sure that what you gather is plentiful, and that gathering it is legal. Remember too that some plants are poisonous to touch. If you don't know a plant, avoid it.

Look beyond weeds and grasses to the pleasing shapes, forms, and colors of lichens, fungi, and mosses. Also, take a fresh look at close-to-home resources in your vegetable garden or produce markets; European arrangers have long appreciated the

voluptuous charm of fruits and vegetables in arrangements. (For example, look at the arrangement on page 91.)

All of these resources, from grasses to peppers, can be augmented or enhanced by the addition of found materials like galls, cones, dried seaweeds, driftwood, seashells, and rocks, which bring more of the outdoors indoors and create original, satisfying effects. Abandon limiting concepts of what constitutes appropriate material for an arrangement, and just look around; even the most mundane objects often reveal treasures for arranging.

Cross-Reference List of Common and Botanical Plant Names

COMMON NAME	BOTANICAL NAME	COMMON NAME	BOTANICAL NAME	COMMON NAME	BOTANICAL NAME
African lily	Agapanthus	**Flowering tobacco**	Nicotiana	**Painted tongue**	Anthurium
Amaryllis	Hippeastrum	**Forget-me-not**	Myosotis	**Pansy**	Viola × wittrockiana
Annual delphinium	Consolida	**Foxglove**	Digitalis	**Peach**	Prunus
Apple	Malus	**Foxtail lily**	Eremurus	**Peony**	Paeonia
Baby's breath	Gypsophila	**Gayfeather**	Liatris	**Persian ranunculus**	Ranunculus
Bachelor's button	Centaurea cyanus	**Geranium**	Pelargonium	**Peruvian lily**	Alstroemeria
Beard tongue	Penstemon	**Globe amaranth**	Gomphrena	**Pincushion flower**	Scabiosa
Bear's breech	Acanthus	**Globe thistle**	Echinops	**Pink**	Dianthus deltoides
Bellflower	Campanula	**Gloriosa lily**	Gloriosa	**Plantain lily**	Hosta
Bells of Ireland	Moluccella	**Grape hyacinth**	Muscari	**Plum**	Prunus
Bird-of-paradise	Strelitzia	**Guernsey lily**	Nerine	**Poinsettia**	Euphorbia pulcherrima
Blanket flower	Gaillardia	**Hawthorn**	Crataegus	**Poor man's orchid**	Schizanthus
Blazing star	Liatris	**Heath**	Erica	**Pot marigold**	Calendula
Bluebell	Scilla	**Hellebore**	Helleborus	**Pussy willow**	Salix caprea
Butterfly flower	Schizanthus	**Holly**	Ilex	**Red-hot poker**	Kniphofia
Calla lily	Zantedeschia aethiopica	**Hollyhock**	Alcea rosea	**Rose**	Rosa
Candytuft	Iberis	**Honesty**	Lunaria	**Scotch heather**	Calluna
Cape jasmine	Gardenia	**Hyacinth**	Hyacinthus	**Sea holly**	Eryngium
Carnation	Dianthus caryophyllus	**Iceland poppy**	Papaver nudicaule	**Sea lavender**	Limonium
Cherry	Prunus	**Ivy**	Hedera helix	**Shasta daisy**	Chrysanthemum maximum
China aster	Callistephus	**Japanese maple**	Acer palmatum		
Chincherinchee	Ornithogalum	**Larkspur**	Consolida	**Snapdragon**	Antirrhinum
Columbine	Aquilegia	**Lavender**	Lavandula	**Squill**	Scilla
Coral bells	Heuchera	**Lilac**	Syringa	**Star-of-Bethlehem**	Ornithogalum
Corkscrew willow	Salix matsudana 'Tortuosa'	**Lily**	Lilium	**Statice**	Limonium
		Lily-of-the-Nile	Agapanthus	**Stock**	Matthiola
Cornflower	Centaurea cyanus	**Lily-of-the-valley**	Convallaria	**Stokes' aster**	Stokesia
Crabapple	Malus	**Lobster claw**	Heliconia	**Strawflower**	Helichrysum
Crown imperial	Fritillaria imperialis	**Lupine**	Lupinus	**Sunflower**	Helianthus
Daffodil	Narcissus	**Madagascar jasmine**	Stephanotis	**Sweet pea**	Lathyrus
Daylily	Hemerocallis	**Marguerite**	Chrysanthemum frutescens	**Sweet violet**	Viola odorata
Desert candle	Eremurus			**Sweet William**	Dianthus barbatus
Dogwood	Cornus	**Marigold**	Tagetes	**Ti**	Cordyline terminalis
False spiraea	Astilbe	**Meadowsweet**	Astilbe	**Torch lily**	Kniphofia
Flamingo flower	Anthurium	**Michaelmas daisy**	Aster	**Transvaal daisy**	Gerbera
Florist's chrysanthemum	Chrysanthemum × morifolium	**Mock orange**	Philadelphus	**Tuberose**	Polianthes
		Money plant	Lunaria	**Tulip**	Tulipa
Flowering cherry	Prunus	**Nasturtium**	Tropaeolum	**Windflower**	Anemone coronaria
Flowering plum	Prunus	**Oriental poppy**	Papaver orientale	**Witch hazel**	Hamamelis
Flowering quince	Chaenomeles	**Ornamental onion**	Allium	**Yarrow**	Achillea

Most arrangements call for a few special
tools and materials. Shown here are florist's
scissors, gloves, a pinholder, smooth pebbles, floral foam, moss, and floral tape.

TOOLS
AND
TECHNIQUES

Whether you grow your own flowers or purchase them from a florist, using the proper techniques and tools for selecting and preparing flowers will greatly increase the beauty and long life of your arrangements.

Before you begin to arrange cut flowers, acquiring some basic information, tools, and materials can increase the design possibilities open to you and ensure that your flowers look, and continue to look, their dazzling best. Special techniques of gathering and preparation will keep your flowers fresh as a garden at dawn. With a little know-how you can have the luxury of spring flowers in the dead of winter. The straightforward procedures described here enable you to preserve many kinds of blossoms, seed structures, and foliage for use and reuse any month of the year. A few simple materials and methods let you place flowers and leaves precisely where you want them in a vase (or a wreath, garland, or corsage) and rest assured that they will stay in place, and in prime condition. Learning about the proper techniques and equipment will help you take full advantage of the bounteous plant materials available in your garden, along roadsides, or at a florist shop.

Gathering, Preparation, and Maintenance

The first steps—properly gathering flowers from your garden or selecting them knowledgeably at a shop, then preparing them to

be arranged—are essential for cut flowers that remain fresh in the vase for as long as possible. Careful maintenance can further extend their freshness. Considering two basic, related facts about cut flowers will help you to appreciate why flowers can't simply be cut or purchased and then arranged without further ado. First, since flower tissues are up to nine-tenths water, keeping them supplied with water and helping them to absorb it are imperative if they are to remain fresh. Second, good hygiene and frequent changes of vase water are crucial to the longevity of cut flowers. The bacteria and fungi that grow in stale vase water decay stem tissues, which results in wilting and early demise of flowers. Most of the following pointers for gathering, preparing, and maintaining flowers are based on these two simple facts.

SELECTING FLOWERS FROM THE GARDEN

With few exceptions, noted in the charts in the previous chapter, select garden flowers just coming into bloom, before any, or much, pollen is loose. For example, choose gladiolus spikes in which only the first three or four blossoms are open, poppies with swelling buds that are starting to slough their outer covering and show color,

You'll quickly learn the value of a florist who sells fresh flowers from sparklingly clean containers.

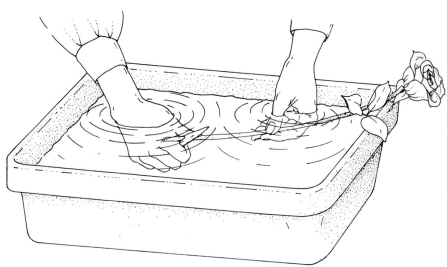

When recutting stems under water, it's only necessary to submerge the portion of the stem end that will be cut.

rosebuds just beginning to unfurl, and daisies whose centers are still hard. Newly opening flowers outlast mature flowers not only because they are younger and sun hasn't faded them but also because wind or insects probably haven't yet pollinated them; many flowers wither quickly once they have fulfilled their reproductive function.

It is also preferable to select flowers that have strong, sturdy stems rather than spindly, scant-blossomed stems from unhealthy plants. Strong, healthy flowers look better, and their vase life is often noticeably longer.

Bear in mind the varying vase lives of different flowers before you gather flowers for an arrangement. An arrangement looks fresh no longer than the vase life of its shortest-lived flower. The vase life of a Southern magnolia blossom might be as brief as one day, but bells of Ireland might last for up to two weeks. Unless you need the arrangement for only a brief time, choose flowers with similar vase lives. For example, to make an arrangement of summer flowers that will look fresh for around a week if properly prepared and maintained, you might choose from among zinnia, penstemon, love-in-a-mist, lavender, statice, gayfeather, baby's breath, gladiolus, fleabane, sweet William, purple coneflower, larkspur, China aster, bellflower, and golden marguerite. If you are planning an arrangement to be used only for a spring party, you might choose from among such relatively short-lived beauties as anemone, hyacinth, forget-me-not, pansy, camellia, lily-of-the-valley, and daphne, as well as longer-lived spring flowers.

GATHERING FLOWERS

The time of day when you gather flowers from the garden is crucial. Midday is least desirable because heat and sunlight have lowered the water content within the plant tissues, and reserves of sugar that contribute to long flower life (see page 46) haven't reached their maximum evening levels. Gathering flowers in the evening takes advantage of high sugar reserves and allows you to condition the flowers overnight, as described below. Gathering in early morning means you can spend less time conditioning because the flower tissues are already well-supplied with water after the cool, moist night. So gather early or late in the day.

Just as important as the gathering time is your method of cutting. Always cut stems with a clean, sharp blade rather than pulling, twisting, or tearing them. Stems damaged by rough treatment are much more susceptible to decay. It's worthwhile to invest in quality cutting tools that will keep a sharp edge for a long time; you'll spend far less time in tool maintenance and repair. Florist's scissors (also called stub scissors) are ideal for cutting soft or moderately firm stems, and well-honed secateurs (pruning shears) are best for cutting woody stems. Leave ample length when cutting stems because often you will need longer stems than you anticipated; it is a simple matter to shorten stems. Slice stems at an angle to maximize water-absorbing surface, and keep the cut surface from resting flat on the bottom of the pail, where absorption of water might be impeded. When you handle flowers during any step, from cutting to arranging, hold them by their stems to avoid damaging blossoms and foliage.

Picturesque as a flower-gathering basket is, a clean pail of tepid water is far kinder to most newly gathered flowers, which wilt quickly unless their stems are immersed in water. Because traces of some metals have adverse effects on various cut flowers, use a plastic, wooden, or enameled pail that has been cleaned thoroughly. Place every stem in water instantly, and keep the pail out of direct sunlight.

A few flowers need immediate, special attention. For example, narcissus and hyacinths should be placed in their own pails for an hour until their sap, which may harm other flowers, has stopped draining. Although most flowers benefit from having their leaves submerged in water, there are a few exceptions.

Flowers with fuzzy or downy foliage (such as dusty miller) should be stripped of any leaves below water level. If fuzzy leaves are submerged they will become waterlogged and will begin to decay. The foliage of certain other flowers also decays rapidly when submerged: stock, marigold, zinnia, aster, China aster, calendula, all species of *Chrysanthemum*, dahlia, blanket flower, and candytuft. Mock orange, lilac, and clematis last longer if all foliage is removed immediately after you gather them. As soon as you've finished cutting, take flowers indoors to be conditioned.

Sharp blades, spotless stem-cutting and conditioning containers, additive, and sheet plastic make for cleanliness and long vase life.

SELECTING FLORIST FLOWERS

When shopping for cut flowers, make sure not only that the blossoms are young and firm, but also that the container water is clear and the stem ends are fresh. Soft or limp buds and blossoms and discolored or drooping foliage indicate that the flowers are old and their period of usefulness to you will be brief. Don't buy roses whose buds are soft and mushy to the touch. Murky container water and discolored, decaying stem ends indicate proliferation of bacteria, which damage plant tissues, impeding water absorption.

Take into account the vase lives of florist flowers when you are buying materials for an arrangement. Be sure that all flowers you select will last for as long as you want the entire arrangement to last. See page 45 and the chart in the previous chapter for information about the vase life of different flowers.

After they have been cut in the fields or greenhouses where they are grown, most florist flowers are quickly placed under refrigeration. The cool, humid conditions of refrigeration reduce the rate at which flowers age, but don't stop the aging process entirely. So flowers refrigerated for long periods of time have aged to some extent. However, because a reliable shop doesn't sell old flowers, and because the flowers it does sell are strong and robust, grown under ideal conditions and free of insect and disease damage, you should find a quality florist shop to supply or supplement

your cut flowers. You can expect to pay more for the higher quality of the flowers and the florist's higher overhead for stocking only the freshest, healthiest flowers, but the extra expenditure is repaid by beautiful, durable flowers.

You may wonder whether street flower stalls, increasingly common in our cities, are good sources of cut flowers. Some are as satisfactory as good florists, if their flowers are fresh and properly prepared, and if they are carefully protected from the elements. However, drying winds, direct sunlight, and temperature extremes often damage the stock in many of these outdoor flower shops.

PREPARATION

Nearly all flowers and foliage look fresher and last longer, in some cases many days longer, if they have been conditioned (sometimes known as being hardened). The conditioning process involves preparing flower tissues so they are filled to capacity with water. Many flowers and foliage plants also need some type of treatment before

they are conditioned that allows them to absorb water efficiently. Without such treatment, the blossoms and leaves of many plants wilt soon after gathering. Flowers from a reliable florist have already been properly treated and conditioned, but if there is any doubt, treat them (if they need special treatment, as described on the following page) before you condition them.

Recutting Stems Under Water

For florist flowers and flowers just brought in from the garden, recutting stems under water is very important for maximizing freshness and vase life. Otherwise, air bubbles may form within the stem tissue and block absorption of water, causing the flowers to wilt. Place the stems under water in a wide container or a sink. Use a sharp, clean, short-bladed knife (or pruners for thick, woody stems) to remove from one to two inches from each stem, cutting at an angle. Then quickly transfer the stem, while the cut end is protected from air by a clinging drop of water, into the container in which the flower will be conditioned, as described on the following page.

FLOWERS WITH MILKY SAP

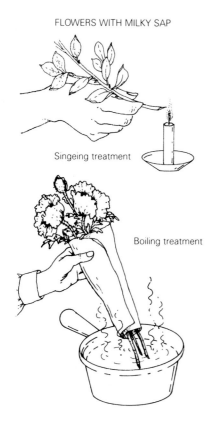

Singeing treatment

Boiling treatment

FLOWERS WITH WOODY STEMS

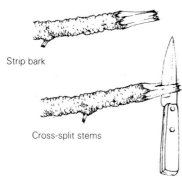

Strip bark

Cross-split stems

FLOWERS WITH HOLLOW STEMS

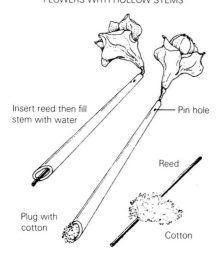

Insert reed then fill stem with water

Pin hole

Plug with cotton

Reed

Cotton

SPECIAL PRECONDITIONING TREATMENTS

Several categories of plants require special treatment before they can be conditioned.

Flowers With Milky Sap

Poinsettias, Oriental poppies, and other flowers with milky sap bleed after cutting, then seal over so they can't absorb water. Just after recutting, singe the stem ends in a candle or gas flame until they blacken to prevent this, or immerse the ends in boiling water for 20 to 30 seconds (poinsettias, however, should be immersed for only a few seconds). Take care that heat doesn't damage foliage or blossoms; devising a shield or wrapping the cut flowers above their stem bases may be necessary. If the stems should need to be recut later, singe or boil the stem ends again.

Flowers With Woody Stems

Trees, shrubs, and many woody and semiwoody perennials such as chrysanthemum require special treatment to facilitate good water absorption. Scrape or cut away the bottom inch of bark with a sharp, short-bladed knife, then split the stem bases 1 to 2 inches high with a knife or sharp pruning shears. A cross split exposes more water-absorbing surface than a single split. The popular practice of hammering woody stem bases may increase absorption at first, but the pulverized tissues are more susceptible to bacterial decay, which results in decreased water absorption. If flowers or leaves have begun to wilt, place split stem ends into hot water (180° F) for a few minutes before conditioning.

Flowers With Hollow Stems

Hollyhocks, amaryllises, delphiniums, large dahlias, and other hollow-stemmed flowers must have their stems filled with water. To do this, turn the stems upside down, pour water into the stems until they are full, and plug the ends with cotton or absorbent floral foam. To eliminate small air bubbles that might be trapped in the stems, pierce the stems just beneath the flower head with a pin, immerse the plugged ends in boiling water for a few seconds, then transfer them to tepid conditioning water. As an added precaution, prevent stems bearing heavy flowers (such as amaryllis) from breaking under the weight of the flower by inserting a stick or reed into the stem before you plug the end.

Conditioning

When you finish recutting each stem under water (and when you finish any special preconditioning treatment), begin instantly to condition—a process that draws as much water as possible into flower and leaf tissues.

Conditioning involves immersing flowers in a clean container of tepid (about 110° F) water. The conditioning water usually contains an additive to prolong vase life, as described below. Immerse flowers almost up to their heads, and immerse most kinds of cut foliage entirely. Most flowers benefit from having their foliage submerged during the conditioning process. The exceptions are those plants with fuzzy foliage, such as dusty miller. Strip all foliage from the bottom third of the stems of fuzzy-leafed plants just before recutting the stems, and condition them in a container filled with enough water to almost reach the lowest leaves. Check the chart beginning on page 22 to determine whether there are special conditioning requirements, such as cold rather than tepid water, for flowers that you cut. Examples of flowers and foliage with special requirements include fern, rhododendron, gardenia, hosta, grape hyacinth, and stock.

For the freshest, longest-lasting flowers and foliage, mix an additive into the conditioning water. The most effective additives are those that supply life-sustaining sugars and prevent or retard the growth of bacteria and fungi in vase water. For more information about additives, see page 46.

Place the containers of flowers or foliage that you are conditioning in a cool, dark, humid place. Basements are often ideal for conditioning, unless there are strong drafts or fumes from a furnace. Leave flowers in their conditioning containers for about eight hours (two at the very least). Then they are ready to be arranged.

When you transfer flowers from conditioning container to vase, strip off all the leaves that will be submerged in water or floral foam, recut the stems under water to the lengths needed for the arrangement, then repeat special treatments for those flowers that require them. This repeated effort might seem unnecessary, but you will find that without it flowers die sooner, sometimes far sooner.

Storing

If you have to delay arranging conditioned flowers for a day or so, simply leave them in the cool, dark place in which you've conditioned them. If you do so, lower the water level if necessary, so that all foliage is above water. Refrigerating flowers is risky. Florists' refrigerators provide a cool, humid atmosphere that retards aging, but air in most home refrigerators is dangerously dry, and flowers can be damaged by the ethylene gas given off by fruit. However, if you have a spare refrigerator, preferably an older, non-self-defrosting type, and if you use it for flowers only, not fruit, you can safely store conditioned flowers in it.

MAXIMIZING VASE LIFE

Proper stem treatment and conditioning, some common-sense maintenance measures, and a few scientifically sound tricks extend the life of cut flowers.

Precautions and Sound Practices

An obvious but easily overlooked life-prolonging measure is to keep the vase filled

Gladioli receive regular conditioning, and tulips are kept in line with plastic wrapping. Fuzzy foliage should stay above water level.

with water. A long-spouted watering can is useful for this purpose. Because plant tissues give off water rapidly, the water level in vases, particularly shallow ones, can plummet. You may be astonished to learn how quickly floral foam can dry out when it sustains flowers whose tissues transpire (give off water) heavily. Check the water level in all vases frequently. This precaution cannot be overemphasized.

Placing the arrangement out of sunlight and away from heat and drafts helps to minimize water loss and retard aging processes. The mantel of a fireplace in use, a table next to a hot south- or west-facing window, a chest near a heating (or air-conditioning) duct, or the top of a warm television set are poor places for cut flowers. For that matter, so is a warm room, especially if it's also dry. Spraying the arrangement periodically helps to slow the rate at which flower tissues lose water—but it may also cause spotting of some blossoms, such as those of many types of orchids. Moving the arrangement to a cool, humid spot during the night slows the destructive effects of a less-than-ideal location.

Good hygiene is imperative; clean vases and utensils are prerequisites for the long vase life of flowers. Scrub dirty stems with a soft brush under warm running water. Sterilize cutting implements and containers before using them. Let a solution of ¼ cup liquid bleach per quart of water stand in well-scrubbed vases for five minutes, then empty and rinse. Immerse scrubbed blades of knives, scissors, or shears in a solution of 1 part bleach to 10 parts water, then rinse thoroughly. Be careful not to splash bleach onto your skin or clothing, or unprotected surfaces.

Changing vase water and cutting stems periodically is a sound practice, though with large arrangements it is difficult and with arrangements in floral foam (which can't be sterilized or reused) it is impossible.

If your tap water is hard—high in mineral salts and therefore harmful to cut flowers—use distilled water. Rainwater can also be used, but only after it has been boiled to kill bacteria. Never use chemically softened water—it harms cut flowers because it contains large quantities of sodium, which is toxic to plant tissues.

Additives

Using additives in vase water (as well as in conditioning water) dramatically increases the vase life of most cut flowers. Most additives work by either increasing the acidity of vase water, which inhibits growth of bacteria, or supplying cut flowers and foliage with sugars that help to sustain life and support growth—including, in the vase, the opening of buds. The best additives both increase acidity of the water and supply sugars.

Vase water with a pH of 3.5 to 4.5 is acidic enough to slow bacterial growth considerably (pH is a measure of acidity). An aspirin tablet can help a bit, though it may make the water too acidic and harm the flowers. A more reliable additive is ¼ teaspoon per gallon of water of citric acid, a compound available at drugstores and chemical supply stores.

One of the most effective killers of bacteria and fungi in vase water is liquid bleach. One-fourth teaspoon of bleach per gallon of water can keep the water clean and sweet for several days.

To nourish flowers and encourage as many buds to open in the vase as possible, add 1 tablespoon of granulated sugar per gallon of vase water. However, because sugar also encourages growth of bacteria, be sure to use bleach or some other germ-discouraging additive as well.

Several ready-made complete additives for cut flowers are widely marketed. These products both disinfect the water and provide sugars. In addition, they reduce the rate at which plant tissues age. You can buy them from most florists.

You can also use tonic water, lemon soda, or lime soda (but not diet soda, which lacks sugar) as additives. Use 2 parts water to 1 part soda or tonic water. The acidity and sugar content of these solutions are ideal for both inhibiting the growth of harmful microbes and providing energy-producing sugars.

Using complete additives or combinations of germicides and sugar solutions is an easy alternative to the effective but sometimes difficult or even impossible practice of cutting stems and changing vase water periodically.

Forcing

On a dark day in late winter, what could be a more sumptuous feast for the senses than an urn of sunny forsythia, a crock of plum blossoms, or a vase of heady lilac? It's easy to get a taste of spring by forcing branches of these and other flowering deciduous shrubs and trees—that is, by stimulating them to bloom or leaf out prematurely indoors.

From mid- to late January or early February, you can begin to force branches gathered from the garden or purchased from a florist. Attempts earlier in the season usually fail because dormant buds haven't had enough chilling. Gather branches on a warm or rainy day when they aren't frozen. Time from cutting to blooming differs from one kind of flower to another and ranges from one to eight weeks. The closer to their natural blooming time that you cut branches, the sooner they will bloom.

Choose heavily budded, substantial stems whenever possible; there's a correlation between stem diameter and quantity of stored sugars present to feed the flower buds. Methods of cutting and preparation are essentially the same as for other cut flowers. With a sharp blade slice branches on a diagonal, cutting so as to shape the plant, not disfigure it. Peel bark back from the bases of the cut stems and split them two or three inches, remove lower twigs, and sink stems into deep containers of water at room temperature (remember that any submerged buds will not open properly). Place the containers in a warm (60° F to 70° F), humid room; a kitchen or large bathroom is often ideal.

The forcing process can sometimes be hurried a bit if you immerse branches in a tub of tepid (around 110° F) water for several hours before transferring them to containers. Change the container water every few days, recutting stems each time you change the water. Add sugar and a few drops of bleach to the water when you change it.

Experiment with any flowering deciduous shrubs and trees that are at hand. The following are proven favorites for forcing: Japanese maple, flowering quince, forsythia, dogwood, hawthorn, daphne, witch hazel, saucer magnolia (and other deciduous magnolias), apple, cherry, plum, almond, crabapple, and other edible and ornamental deciduous fruit trees, mock orange, pussy willow, and spiraea. Wisteria, a woody vine, also forces easily.

Preserving

Their special loveliness and practicality suit preserved flowers to any interior. Dried or treated blossoms, seed structures, and foliage vastly expand a flower arranger's repertoire. Some preserved flowers bring indoors the mellowness of Indian summer. Others lend touches of natural grace and color appropriate for any season.

All preserved materials look at home in rustic interiors with natural wood, unfinished brick, or earthy tones. In formal period interiors, dried flowers can add appropriate elegance, as demonstrated by the arrangement on page 84. A container of dried wild grasses or large-scale weeds or a simple bunch of dried wheat can complement even the most austere of contemporary interiors.

Preserved flowers are becoming available commercially, sold in bunches or as individual stems. However, preserving your own gives you far greater variety. Many plant materials can be preserved, often by more than one method. The charts in the previous chapter tell which plants you can preserve most successfully, and indicate what methods to use to preserve them.

After several weeks, forced branches of pussy willow and flowering plum burst into bloom.

PREDRIED PLANTS

Some of the most resplendent materials for preserved-flower arrangements can easily be gathered predried and ready to use from the humblest places. Make a habit of scanning vacant lots and roadsides for the myriad handsome "weeds," like Queen Anne's lace, fennel, dock, horsetail, pearly everlasting, sedge, teasel, cattail, thistle, and cow parsnip; by late summer or early autumn they are dry and not yet beaten down by storms. Most of their blossoms and leaves will have withered or fallen away to expose the stark, elegant architecture of the plant. Many wild grasses, too, make excellent predried materials for your arrangements.

Remove any unsightly withered foliage from weeds and grasses, as well as easily dispersed seeds that have no decorative value. Spray still-intact cattails and fluffy grasses with hair spray to keep them from shedding their fluff. Similarly, collect stems bearing fluffy seed parts, such as clematis, when they look their best, and coat them on the spot with hair spray.

FRESH PLANTS

When choosing fresh flowers, foliage, and other materials to preserve from your garden, the wilds, or the florist, bear in mind the following pointers.

Be very selective when gathering fresh flowers. Distortions, holes, spots, and other imperfections in damaged flowers and other plant materials are exaggerated by preserving, and you might have to live with the flaws for a long time.

Gather blossoms that haven't yet passed their prime. Otherwise, they might drop petals or the entire blooms may shatter. For natural variety in your arrangements, you'll probably also want to gather buds at various stages of development, and seed pods. Gather only fully mature foliage for glycerine treatment; immature plant tissue doesn't preserve well. Check carefully to make sure that all fresh flowers and any leaves that you want to preserve are firm and unwilted. If necessary, condition them before drying or glycerinating them. Cut grasses just before they come into bloom (before they produce pollen). Grains like rye and wheat may be cut later, after they've bloomed but while they're still green. Many seed structures can be gathered any time before or after they've dried naturally on the plants.

Collect plant materials for air-drying or dessication in midday or afternoon, in dry weather. Dampness encourages mold and slows the drying process. As a rule, the slower the flowers dry, the less your chance of preserving bright or delicate colors.

When possible, gather more than you need; since many preserved flowers are fragile, there will probably be some casualties. Remember that it may be up to a year before you can gather and preserve more of the same kind of flower.

Though most air-dried plants are hung to dry, some, like heather, are stood upright in a small amount of water that is allowed to evaporate.

For flower heads atop weak stems or stems that tend to wither during drying, cut the stem so that only an inch remains beneath each head, then wire each flower head before you dry it, as shown on page 55. If you try to wire the flowers after they've been dried, they will be brittle and fragile and will shatter easily. If you intend to use dessicants, it's usually best to cut the stems off of all flowers, leaving only a small portion attached to each blossom. This is because dessicating whole stems requires great quantities of dessicant and huge treatment containers in order to position flower heads upright. You can air-dry suitable stems, like those of daylily, yarrow, and delphinium, and then attach the dessicated, wired flower heads to the dried stems with wire and tape, or you can simply wrap the wires with floral tape to form false stems.

AIR-DRYING

Air-drying is the simplest, most popular method of preserving blossoms, foliage, and seed structures. This technique requires only a spot in the attic, beneath indoor stairs, or any well-ventilated, dark or dimly lit place where there is room to hang bunches of flowers to dry. Some living areas are greatly enhanced by bunches of drying flowers hanging from beams or racks; their decorative value is illustrated in the photograph on the opposite page.

Remove foliage from stems, unless it will dry attractively, and gather a few stems into a bunch, arranging them loosely enough so that the flower heads don't crowd one another.

Flowers that are dried quickly will retain the most color. To this end, it's especially important to remove unwanted leaves and side stems that you would later discard anyway, because they can lower the quality of the dried flowers by slowing the drying process. Similarly, in large, crowded bunches the drying process is considerably slower, so the flowers are more likely to fade during drying.

Tie the stems securely but don't crush them; rubber bands are useful for keeping bunches intact as the stems dry and shrink. Hang the bunches upside down, far enough apart to permit air to circulate. Under ideal conditions the most delicate plants dry in about a week and most others in two to three weeks. Thick-stemmed, heavy materials may take twice as long, however, so be especially careful to dry them in small, widely separated bunches.

Some air-dried flowers require special techniques. Delphinium and hydrangea keep their color better if dried very quickly in hot air, perhaps close to a heater or in a hot attic. Upright rather than upside-down drying is preferable for most plants with sturdy upright stems and round, many-spoked flower heads, such as fennel, Queen Anne's lace, and dill, as well as eucalyptus and delicate or fluffy grasses. Some flower stems should be stood upright in a half-inch of water, which is then allowed to evaporate as the flowers dry. Flowers that should be dried this way include hydrangea, heather, flossflower, bells of Ireland, yarrow, and the majority of grasses.

You can store flowers where you've dried them as long as the spot is dark, the air remains dry, and moths and rodents don't attack the flowers. Otherwise, store them carefully in closed boxes in a dry place. Use mothballs if necessary. If humidity is a problem, use an airtight container with a little bag of silica gel crystals inside (see next page); if air can enter around the lid, seal it with nonporous tape.

DRYING WITH DESSICANTS

Instead of air-drying some flowers, you may decide to use dessicants—substances that draw moisture out of plant tissues. Their chief advantage over air-drying is superior retention of flower color and, in many cases, of original flower shape. When gathering fresh blossoms for dessication, make sure that they are perfectly dry, because even a drop of dew can cause the dessicant to stick to a flower and ruin it.

The procedures for using most dessicants are similar. Start by wiring the flower heads (see page 55). Fill airtight containers with at least 1 inch of dessicant. Set the wired flowers on the dessicant and carefully cover them with more dessicant until they are completely buried. The weight of the dessicant may cause flowers to flatten out as they dry. To prevent this, invert flowers with only one or two rows of petals (like daisies) on small mounds of dessicant. The mound will support the natural shape of the flower even after the remainder of the dessicant is added. Many-petaled flowers, such as roses, require a different procedure. Make a shallow depression in the dessicant and place the flower in the depression right side up. To avoid damaging petals, add the rest of the dessicant with extreme care. Gently sift the dessicant through your fingers onto the flowers, or spoon the dessicant against the inside of the container. It will gradually slide up and over the petals without damaging them. Then close the container until the flowers are dry.

Flowers buried in dessicant should never overlap or even touch one another; it's best to leave a space of 3 inches or more between flowers so moisture from one flower will not seep to another. It's a good idea to place flowers of the same kind in the same container rather than mixing different kinds of flowers. This will ensure that the flowers in each container will all dry at about the same rate.

To determine if flowers are dry, slowly tilt the container until enough dessicant slides away so that some of the petal tips are exposed. Carefully feel them. If the petals are crisp and papery, they're dry. If they're still soft, re-cover them with dessicant and check again in a day or so. Remove dried flowers by slowly pouring out the dessicant until you can pick them out by their stems.

Store dessicant-preserved flowers in closed containers and protect them from pests and high humidity. Flowers with stems can be stored by standing them upright in jars or sticking them into blocks of rigid plastic foam such as Styrofoam then enclosing them in large containers. They can also be stored by burying them carefully in clean, dry sand.

Silica Gel

Silica gel is a quick dessicant, drying most flowers in two to three days (fleshy flowers, like lilies, can take up to ten days). It is therefore excellent for retaining clear, vivid colors (though some hues change). Many people experienced in using dessicants favor silica gel because of the outstanding results that they achieve with it.

Although silica gel costs more than other dessicants, it can be reused indefinitely, so there is only an initial investment. The grade of silica gel crystal used to dessicate flowers is fine, almost powdery. You can buy silica gel crystals from a florist, flower supply or crafts shop, nursery, or chemical supply company, under various trade names. Crystals are blue when dry and pink or white when damp. Always oven-dry pink or white crystals in a shallow baking pan at 250° F until they turn blue, and cool the crystals before reusing. Store silica gel crystals in an airtight container.

After drying, remove the flowers from the silica gel crystals right away; leaving them too long makes them impossibly dry and fragile. A broken petal can usually be reattached with a small drop of glue. Use a soft artist's brush to remove any powder that clings to petals.

Borax

Borax, either pure or mixed with an equal volume of cornmeal, is used like silica gel but has the advantage of extreme lightness, which suits it particularly to delicate, fine-textured plant materials rather than large, substantial flowers. Drying time is usually somewhere between 2 and 10 days; check frequently to determine when flowers are dry so you can remove them before the petals begin to spot. Brushing borax from petals is difficult and requires diligence; be sure to remove every trace to prevent spotting.

Sand

Fine sand is a useful dessicant, as long as it has been properly prepared. Wash it thoroughly and strain it if necessary to remove ocean salt or any organic materials. Bake it in a shallow tray at 259° F to dry it and kill any microorganisms. To be sure the sand is completely dry, mix some silica gel crystals into it before you bake it; the crystals will turn blue when the sand is dry. Sift the dried sand to break up lumps. Because of its heaviness, sand is unsuitable for very delicate materials. It is, however, well suited to flowers like dahlias and peonies whose petals wrinkle when dried with a light dessicant. It is easier to fill thoroughly between petals and in crevices with sand than with other dessicants. Place plant materials on a 1- to 2-inch layer of sand, then cover them with more sand, in the same manner described under "Silica Gel," above. It is not necessary to seal the container. Drying time ranges from several days to four weeks. With sand, there's no danger of leaving flowers covered too long.

MICROWAVE DRYING

Microwave drying of plant materials covered with a dessicant, preferably silica gel, is the newest and by far the fastest method of drying. Because it is so fast, when it works well the natural colors of the flowers undergo surprisingly little change. Microwave drying works extremely well for most, though not for all, flowers; even blossoms of varieties that usually dry perfectly by this method may turn out poorly if their water content is abnormally low when the drying process is begun.

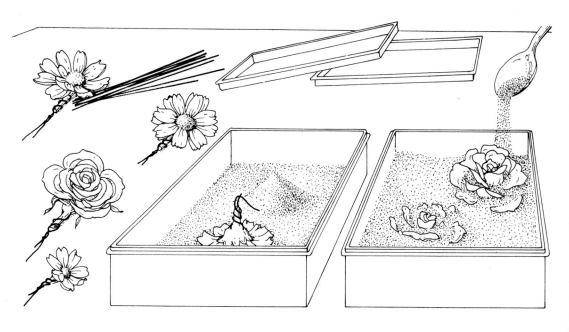

Daisies retain their form best if they are inverted over mounds of dessicant. Place roses and other multi-petaled flowers upright, and gently cover them with dessicant.

Combined with yarrow, delphinium, oak, and other dried materials in this arrangement are glycerinated eucalyptus leaves. They differ markedly in color from the fresh leaves in the foreground.

Among the flowers best suited to microwave drying are anemones, pansies, roses, chrysanthemums, tulips, carnations, Dutch irises, some of the fleshier orchids, dogwoods, marigolds, and peonies. Extremely small, fine-textured or delicate flowers tend to dry least successfully by this method.

Use the following guidelines for microwave drying—but experiment with all flowers at hand and with different microwave settings. Try variations on the techniques set forth here. Because microwave drying provides almost instant results, some experimentation can teach you a great deal.

First, preheat the silica gel in the microwave on a high setting until its crystals turn bright blue; this should take about a minute. Then fill a plastic or ovenproof glass container with an inch of the warm silica gel crystals. You may want to dry only one flower at a time to minimize the time that each flower stays in the oven, in order to get truer color and to avoid losing more than one flower if adjustments are needed. If you dry more than one flower at a time, space the flowers 2 to 3 inches apart. Use flowers just reaching their prime; condition them if their tissues need more water.

Place each blossom on the bed of warm silica gel crystals in the same way you would position it in a dessicant if you were not using the microwave (see previous page). Carefully cover the flower with the silica gel crystals so they fill thoroughly between the petals. Make sure the flower isn't flattened, crushed, or otherwise distorted. Set the timer for between 1 and 3½ minutes, depending on the thickness of the flower petals.

If you find that the oven dries the flowers unevenly, you may want to interrupt the drying every 30 seconds to rotate

Among the materials and tools for arranging are: floral foams (green for arranging stems in water, and brown for dried arrangements), Styrofoam plastic foam, floral tape, paddle wire, wire cutters, and florist's clay (here coiled in white waxed paper), as well as chicken wire, mosses to hide mechanics, a watering can, a long knife, a bottle brush, a sprayer, and a pinholder.

the container; using a microwave oven with a rotating rack avoids this problem. If flowers are consistently so dry and brittle that their petals break when you remove them from the silica gel crystals, try placing a dish of water in the oven along with the container of silica gel crystals.

After removing the container from the oven, let it stand for 20 to 30 minutes before gently pouring away the crystals and removing the flower.

TREATING WITH GLYCERINE

The best preservative for many kinds of leaves, especially coarse ones, as well as for berries, is glycerine. This liquid chemical is available at most pharmacies but is usually far less expensive when purchased from chemical supply companies. Glycerine provides a useful alternative to other dessicants, even for leaves that can be just as effectively preserved by air-drying methods, because it often alters foliage colors in an interesting manner. Green foliage frequently changes to rich, autumnal reds, browns, bronzes, and yellows. The nature and extent of the color changes depend not just on the kind of plant, but on the season in which it's gathered and sometimes on the length of time the material is treated with glycerine. The hues of naturally reddish or bronze foliage and most berries change little, however. Glycerine works by

replacing the water in plant tissues rather than by removing it, so stems and leaves stay supple and berries stay smooth and firm indefinitely. Most glycerinated plant materials remain in prime condition for years if they are stored upright, with their stems in cans or jars, and covered. Dusty glycerinated materials can easily be restored to their original glycerinated color if they are cleaned by washing with soap and warm water.

Gather stems of mature foliage and fresh, firmly attached berries just as you would gather them for fresh arrangements. Young, immature leaves and soft, new shoots wilt and collapse in glycerine solution because they haven't yet developed rigid tissues. Gathering in mid- to late summer is a good idea, but by early autumn deciduous leaves have begun to loosen from their stems.

Remove dust and dirt from all cut materials. Cut all stems on the diagonal. Scrape bark from the bottom 3 or 4 inches of woody stems and split or crush the ends to maximize absorptive surface. Immerse the stems to a depth of 5 or 6 inches in a well-mixed solution of 1 part glycerine and 2 parts boiling water, then let the glycerine solution cool. Check the level during the treatment and add more solution as necessary. This treatment should last three to seven days for plants with soft stems and one to six weeks for woody plants. Leaves that are thick and leathery, such as the leaves of Southern magnolia, will absorb the glycerine solution at a slow rate. To speed the process, wipe the leaves with some of the solution. Glycerine solution usually won't move out to the tips of stems longer than about 16 inches, so wiping leaves with glycerine solution is especially helpful in preserving leaves toward the tips of the branches or stems.

Remove the stems from the solution when beads of moisture form on leaf surfaces, colors change out to the tips of leaves, and the undersides of leaves become oily. Be careful to remove soft-tissued plants before they become limp. Wipe leaves and stems dry with absorbent tissue. If leaves toward the tips of branches are droopy rather than firm after treatment, hang the branches upside down to help draw the solution to the tips. Save the glycerine solution for reuse; a few drops of bleach will keep it from mildewing. If the solution turns dark, it will be no less effective than when it was clear.

Equipment, Containers, and Mechanics

By the time you gather fresh flowers or prepare preserved ones and bring them to your work table, you'll probably have a general idea of how you want to arrange them. But without some utilitarian materials and a little forethought about their use, you may waste flowers or fail to actualize design ideas, or both. So have your work space, tools and equipment, containers, and mechanics at hand and understand their functions before you start designing.

WORKING SPACE, TOOLS, AND OTHER EQUIPMENT

The place in which you prepare and arrange flowers may be large and elaborate or compact and minimally equipped, depending on the layout of your house and the extent of your involvement in flower arranging. Consider the features of an ideal working space discussed here, then try to incorporate as many of these features as possible into your own space.

The ideal space is out of the way of heavy foot traffic and constant distractions. Counter or tabletop space is ample, and there is room for you to move freely about. Storage spaces for tools, containers, and other equipment are close at hand. A sink, preferably a double one, is nearby. Lighting is excellent (daylight and incandescent lighting don't distort colors). There is protection from hot sun, high temperatures, strong drafts, and dry air. Disposal of debris is easy. Surfaces are easy to clean and keep sanitary. The area you use to condition flowers is nearby. Not least important, the working atmosphere is conducive to creativity. Even if you don't have a special setup for arranging flowers, with a few additions your kitchen counter or utility room table can effectively double as work space.

The same implements you've used for gathering flowers and foliage together with a few other pieces of equipment, serve you well as you proceed to arrange what you've gathered. Sharp, clean cutting tools for all types of plant materials—a small knife, florist's scissors, and secateurs (pruning shears)—are basic necessities. A sharp, long-bladed knife is handy for cutting into blocks of floral foam. Unless the blades of your floral scissors are notched for cutting wire, you will probably need a wire cutter; even the finest wire ruins scissors and shears. A thorn remover for rose stems spares your hands and makes rose stems easier to arrange, but it damages the bark of stems and may hasten their deterioration. It's also helpful to have on hand a bottle brush for scrubbing narrow, deep containers, a long-spouted watering can for adding water to flower-filled vases, and a sheet of plastic to protect surfaces if necessary and to simplify cleaning up.

VASES AND OTHER CONTAINERS TO HOLD ARRANGEMENTS

For making arrangements, vases or other containers are a basic necessity. On page 69 you'll find design-oriented ideas about containers. But here our concerns are purely practical.

Don't limit the possibilities to vases. Any vessel is a potential container, and for preserved materials, which don't require water, baskets can be admirably suitable. (Because preserved materials may be top-heavy in a basket or other lightweight container, be sure to use sterilized sand, rocks, pennies—anything that can function as ballast.) For fresh arrangements, plastic or glass containers of various shapes and sizes are invaluable as liners for "vases" as diverse as baskets and dried gourds.

When you know what types of arrangements you'll make—not that your repertoire won't grow and change in time—you'll know what container shapes and sizes you need to hold the flowers and foliage. Possibilities range from platters and bowls to tall cylinders, from urns or lined pails to simple bud vases.

A word of caution here: Many unglazed ceramic containers, unless their inside surfaces are glazed, seep moisture (for example, most terra-cotta ware will do this). To avoid damaging wood furniture, set such containers on dishes or other waterproof bases, or use liners inside them, since seeping water eventually makes unsightly mineral deposits on container surfaces.

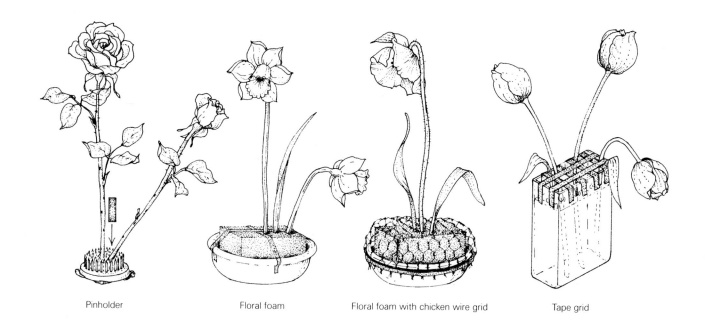

Pinholder　　　　Floral foam　　　　Floral foam with chicken wire grid　　　　Tape grid

MECHANICS

Mechanics are the devices used to hold flowers in place. Many beautiful arrangements in the informal styles popular today are constructed without mechanics. However, design possibilities are greatly increased by the use of mechanics. The following materials and devices are widely available and are especially useful for positioning flowers securely.

Pinholders (often known by their Japanese name *kenzan*) of various sizes and shapes allow you to impale stem ends securely on sharp, closely spaced spikes. Some pinholders have an outer cage that offers further support to heavy stems. Others are designed as shallow, water-holding wells, especially useful in very shallow containers. Pinholders with bases of heavy metal are more stable than lighter, cheaper ones, though all can be anchored to their containers with florist's clay.

Wire netting, an old favorite with arrangers, can be chicken wire, or a more pliable and durable coated netting sold specifically for flower arranging. Tightly crumpled netting stuffed into an open container lets you position stems, but the wires sometimes get in the way and make it difficult to place stems exactly where you want them. Wire netting is more useful

stretched over the mouth of a container, fashioned into widely spaced, crumpled layers, or cupped over or pressed into a pinholder. Waterproof florist's tape can anchor it securely to the rim or the inside of a container.

Floral foam can extend design possibilities enormously. Rigid plastic foam such as Styrofoam, and floral foam made expressly for preserved materials, are a boon to the arranger of dried or glycerine-treated flowers. Water-retentive foams for fresh flowers come in blocks or cylinders that can be cut to fit nearly any container. Some are available in different densities, for either normal or very tender stems. If the stems aren't rigid enough to insert into the foam, use a pencil or a stick to make holes for them. Foams are usually anchored to their containers with waterproof tape. Wire mesh placed over foam and taped to the container provides further support for heavy stems. Some floral foams are sold in ready-made holders that can be anchored like pinholders. Others are designed to extend above the rim of the container, allowing you to angle stems downward when inserting them into the foam. All supply ample water to plant materials as long as the foam has been saturated before use and is kept standing in water. However, if one brick of foam is stacked atop another

brick, leaving it above water level, water will not be drawn from the vase to the upper brick and it will dry out. Because some types of floral foam are fairly costly, it's tempting to reuse them. This is not a good practice, however. Eventually, foams begin to disintegrate, new stems fit imperfectly in old holes, resulting in air pockets, and reused foam harbors bacteria and fungi. Discard absorbent floral foam after using it once.

Waterproof adhesive tape is invaluable for anchoring foam. Occasionally, it is used to make a grid over the mouth of a container to support stems, sometimes with the added help of a pinholder secured to the base of the container. Like many other mechanics, tape can be camouflaged with foliage.

Floral binding tape is a flexible, stretchy tape available in green, brownish green, white, and other colors. Floral tape is often used together with wire to reinforce stems or to make false stems for flowers used in corsages, nosegays, bouquets, and dried arrangements. It is available in various widths; the half-inch width is best for most uses.

Florist's wire, available in several gauges, in short lengths or on reels, serves a range of stabilizing purposes. Some wire is laminated with a plastic green coating to

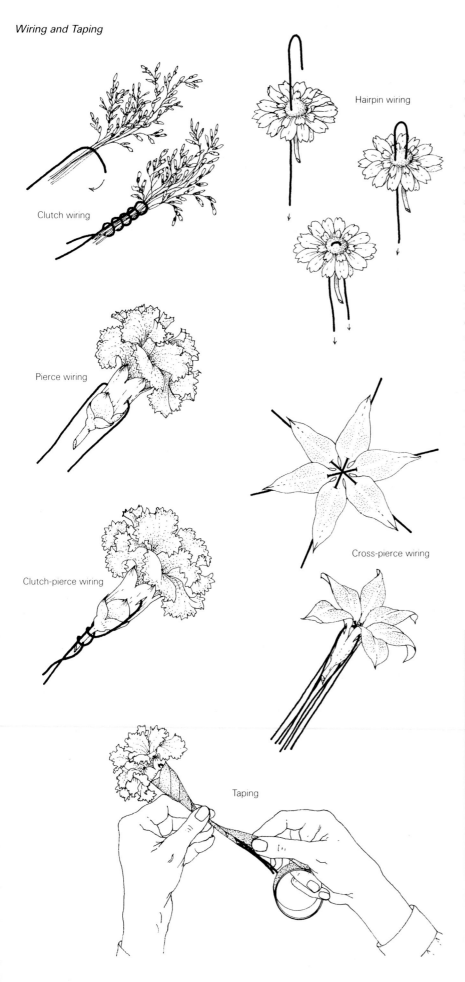

Clutch wiring

Hairpin wiring

Pierce wiring

Clutch-pierce wiring

Cross-pierce wiring

Taping

camouflage it and to retard rusting. Wire can be wrapped around the stems of fresh or dried flowers to strengthen them, or it can be run lengthwise through weak stems of fresh flowers (though this method isn't conducive to their long life). Wire together with tape is indispensable for making corsages and other floral decorations. Wire on reels, sometimes called paddle wire, is used for garlands and wreaths.

Clean pebbles, gravel, marbles, shells, and sterile sand provide an easy means of stabilizing stems in a vase. Polished pebbles, shells, and marbles can add a decorative element to the arrangement when used in clear glass containers. All can be used as ballast for fresh or dried arrangements that are top-heavy. Sand or fine gravel can be used to raise the level of a pinholder or absorbent foam in a deep container, as long as the pinholder or foam can be anchored securely to the sides of the container.

Cones, also called funnels or tubes, are helpful in making massive arrangements in which some flowers must be raised so high that, without the water-containing cones, they would have no water supply. The cones are attached to long sticks. The scale of arrangements for the home, however, seldom requires the use of cones.

Flowers for Special Occasions

Bouquets and nosegays, boutonnieres and corsages make their appearance most often at weddings and other formal occasions. Evergreen garlands and wreaths are traditional Christmas decorations. All of these floral constructions require more mechanics than most arrangements. With practice, though, you'll be able to make your own corsages, nosegays, and other decorations for special occasions. The adjacent photograph shows traditional bridal white combined with holiday red and green in a boutonniere, corsage, nosegay, and wreath, creating a festive color scheme for a Christmas wedding. You can use any kind of flower and color scheme in making all of these constructions.

The wreath, corsage, boutonniere, and nosegay are for a Christmas wedding. Here, fruit and greenery are combined with narcissus, stephanotis, lily-of-the-valley, chincherinchee, freesia, and tulip.

BOUTONNIERE

1. Loosely arrange the materials in your hand to determine how the finished boutonniere will appear.

2. Wire and tape the individual components, as shown on page 55.

3. Arrange the materials again, then tape them together to make the completed boutonniere.

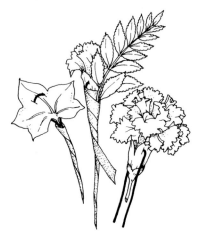

CORSAGE

1. Arrange the materials loosely in your hand or on a table surface. To make a corsage with a pointed oval shape place the smallest bud at the top of the corsage, then arrange the remaining buds and flowers according to size, from the smallest to the largest. Remove any unwanted buds and flowers from clusters or sprays.

2. Wire and tape each leaf, berry, flower, or cluster separately, as shown on page 55, taping foliage and fine-textured flowers such as baby's breath or lily-of-the-valley to each stem as you work. Make each false stem about 6 inches long.

3. Starting with the topmost bud and alternating sides as you move downward, attach each component with a piece of tape to the main stem that you are creating. Be sure to build a slight curve into the corsage so it will fit the contour of the body.

4. As you tape each flower onto the main stem, angle the flower downward slightly so that it will point toward the viewer rather than upward. After you have added the last flower, wind the tape ten times or so around the joining point. You can wire the bow into the corsage at any time before it is completed, or you can tie it on after the corsage is finished. The bow should accent rather than dominate the design. Cut individual stems at approximately but not precisely the same length.

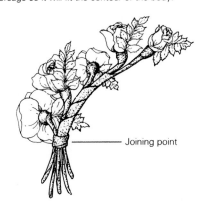

Joining point

NOSEGAY AND BOUQUET

Although a corsage is one-sided and nosegays and bouquets are rounded, their construction is essentially the same. For a nosegay or bouquet, wire and tape individual stems, then tape them together at the joining point, just as you would with a corsage, and add a bow, perhaps with streamers. For another way to make a nosegay or bouquet, read about making a hand-tied bouquet on page 87.

GARLANDS AND WREATHS

1. The process of making garlands is similar to that of making wreaths. To make a garland, unroll a couple of feet of wire from a spool of paddle wire. Use the end of this leading wire, which will be the spine of the garland, to clutch-wire a tip of greenery.

2. Use a continuous piece of wire of the same gauge from a second spool—this is the wrapping wire—to attach more sprigs of greenery to the leading wire, alternating sides. Instead of discarding them, use any blunt-tipped greenery you have to fill in the garland. Save portions with tips for places where they will show, to give the garland a natural look.

3. To make a wreath, use a rigid wire frame (available at floral supply stores and many garden centers), or make your own frame by bending a heavy wire coat hanger into a circle. The frame performs the same function as the leading wire in a garland. Attach sprigs of greenery to the frame by clutch-wiring them.

4. Decorate wreaths and garlands by attaching wired pinecones, fruit, flowers, and ribbons to them.

5. Tie the wire securely underneath the wreath or garland and clip off the ends.

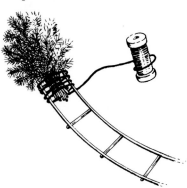

Utter simplicity characterizes this dramatic arrangement of agapanthus. The design is Western, but strong Eastern influence is evident in the linear, asymmetrical form and in the use of rock and polished pebbles.

DESIGNING WITH FLOWERS

Whether you're placing a few flowers in a simple container, or creating a formal centerpiece for a dinner party, understanding design basics will help ensure a pleasing arrangement that fits well into its surroundings.

Styles of flower arranging, like styles in other arts, have undergone constant change over the years. Traditional styles or modern adaptations of them, particularly useful for formal settings and occasions, remain a part of many a flower arranger's repertoire. Styles of everyday arrangements, however, have become more spontaneous, natural, and individualized, reflecting the way we live. A casual jar of wild grasses, for example, has more currency in modern everyday life than a large, meticulously contrived floral construction.

Increasingly, American and European flower arrangers are bending or even disregarding traditional rules and guidelines. As you gain experience in arranging flowers, you will probably come to feel that designing with flowers has more to do with using flowers flexibly to achieve the look you want than with following a strict formula. You will also find that the more you train your eye to see, the more subtle and pleasing the design you can create with cut flowers.

One of the surest ways to train your eye is to understand the traditional principles of arranging. Many of the most basic principles of floral design are actually adaptations of general design principles, applicable to any kind of design, including architecture and interior design. These basic design principles transcend trends and fashions.

You will find that the ultimate teacher is nature itself. Through close, constant observation of design in nature, your own floral designs will gain in subtlety and grace. Make it a habit to notice how plants look and how they grow. Pay attention to how different kinds of plants hold their blossoms, leaves, and stems; exactly how each part catches the light; what patterns, textures, and colors the blossoms, stems and leaves, and bark display, and in what combinations; how plants develop and change in color and form through a season; which plants look best together; and how many shades of green exist in even the smallest plot of vegetation. The visual aspects of plants in nature are subtle and diverse. Just look, and continue to look. Develop a discerning eye.

Approach flower arranging in a relaxed (but not careless), experimental, even playful spirit. To neglect enjoyment in arranging flowers is to miss much of the point. This positive attitude, together with a visual appreciation of plants and an understanding of basic design principles, can help you to develop your skills in floral design to the level of an individualized and immensely satisfying art.

A primary purpose of this book, and the specific aim of this chapter, is to advance you in a direction that will both provide immediate satisfaction and lead you to richer rewards as you gain experience.

A stem of lily and two sprigs of ivy in a gracefully shaped and proportioned glass vase harmonize with the sophisticated setting.

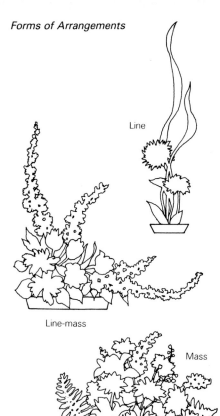

Line

Line-mass

Mass

Some Shapes of Mass Arrangements

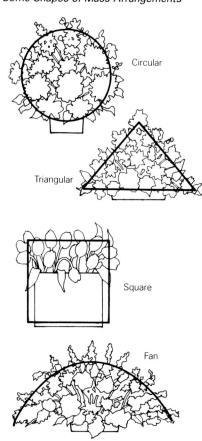

Circular

Triangular

Square

Fan

Toward that end, the rest of this chapter discusses possibilities and gives guidelines in three broad aspects of floral design: the forms that arrangements can take, the functions and interrelationships of color and texture, and the context in which an arrangement appears.

Forms

No matter what its style or how elaborate it is, every arrangement has an overall form, or shape. There are two aspects to the form of an arrangement: its outline or silhouette, and the individual forms of its component materials.

OVERALL FORMS

The traditional concepts of form in floral arrangement have a historical basis (see pages 5 to 7 for a brief history of flower arranging). The traditional concepts reflect Oriental as well as traditional European designs, and the more recently developed designs of the past several decades are a blend of both.

Line Arrangements

The ikebana arrangement in the upright vase, pictured and discussed on pages 78 and 79, is an example of a line arrangement. The linear plant materials determine the overall shape of the arrangement. (See "Forms Within a Traditional Arrangement," on page 62.) In this arrangement, three branches of forsythia radiate outward, both above and below the rim of the vase, to make a clear-cut, simple shape or silhouette. Open spaces between the lines are as much a part of the form as the lines themselves. On page 58 you will find a line arrangement that is contemporary American, though Oriental influence is obviously strong. Line arrangements are usually made to be viewed from only one side.

Mass Arrangements

The traditional European floral design, unlike the Oriental or Oriental-inspired design, has a solid or nearly solid outline. "Bouquet," which derives from Old French words meaning "thicket," "clump," or "forest," is the term used to designate a typical mass arrangement. The Dutch painting shown on page 6 depicts an opulent "thicket" of flowers. Many modern American styles, whether lush and solid or loose and airy, derive from this historical European concept of massed flowers. The majority of arrangements pictured in this book fall into the category of mass arrangements. Some have been designed to be viewed in the round, and others have fronts and backs, but all have solid or nearly solid silhouettes that define their particular shapes. The most common shapes of the mass arrangements pictured in this book are fans, circles, ovals, and triangles, though many of these shapes are muted in form rather than precisely geometric. Their indistinctness reflects the modern trend away from stark geometry, toward shapes whose geometry is more subtle and natural looking.

Line-Mass Arrangements

It was probably inevitable, once ikebana had been introduced to Europe and America, that a form would develop combining the concepts of mass and line. Line-mass designs became popular in the first half of the twentieth century. Their shapes are defined mainly by lines, but the lines are fleshed out with flowers and foliage, so that the overall form falls midway between line and mass. Some have geometric shapes, such as crescents, columns, slender or "pronged" triangles, and S-curves. An example of a line-mass design is the nearly columnar arrangement beside a mirrored bathroom wall on the opposite page. Striking line-mass arrangements with a contemporary feel are still made today, but the stiff line-mass triangles so popular a few decades ago are now outmoded.

Corkscrew willow
and slender stems of
bellflower create a
strong linear element
in this contemporary
line-mass
arrangement.

Perfect proportion and balance characterize a graceful arrangement of false spiraea, roses, elderberries, Japanese anemone seed heads, and Stevia.

Plant materials in most traditional mass and line-mass arrangements and in many contemporary floral designs are divided into three categories. Each category is determined by the plant's form within the arrangement—that is, by the way the plant's overall shape allows it to function within the design. As you will recognize, some plant materials can function differently in different styles of arrangements. For example, irises can be used as focal materials in one design and line materials in another.

Line Materials

Long-stemmed, elongated flower spikes, long swordlike leaves, or branches are used to establish the basic structural lines of many traditional arrangements, including line, mass, and line-mass arrangements. Line materials are placed so that they rise up and outward from the center of the vase to define the outermost point in the outline as well as the central axis and other prominent lines. The *central axis* is the tallest and most prominent line, and its tip should be positioned directly above the center of the composition. The branch, leaf, or flower that is placed to form the central axis is often selected for its graceful lines and detail.

Classic examples of line materials include gladiolus, plum, pussy willow, forsythia, iris, larkspur, and foxtail lily. Because they define the overall structure of the arrangement, position line materials in the container before adding the other materials.

Focal Materials

The focal materials are usually large, rounded blossoms but may also be foliage or even vegetables or fruit. Focal materials compose the center or centers of attention in a traditional arrangement. Added after the line materials, they join the lines together. Usually they are concentrated above the rim of the vase, in the middle rather then at the fringes of the arrangement. Among the innumerable possibilities for focal materials are roses, lilies, carnations, large individual orchids (rather than sprays), tulips, large chrysanthemums, dahlias, gerberas, and large daisies.

Filler

Added after the line and focal materials, fillers soften, enrich, and round out many mass and line-mass designs. They are often flowers, usually small, clustered ones. Some of the classic fillers include baby's breath, heather, and statice. Leaves—large or small, fine or bold—and smaller individual blossoms often serve this function, as do berries, catkins, stems of grass, and bud clusters.

FORM DYNAMICS

The forms within many arrangements lead the eye around the arrangement. Often, arrangements are designed so that the eye moves along the central axis and the other line materials toward the focal materials, where it comes to rest. In addition, form often balances against form, creating rhythms that can make the difference between floral compositions that are pleasingly lively, or ones that are lifeless and even dissonant. These concepts apply to most traditional styles of design, though some are equally applicable to many of the most contemporary concepts.

Focus

As discussed above in connection with focal materials, many traditional designs have large, rounded flowers concentrated just above the rim of the vase, where lines converge. This is the *focal area* or *central focus* of the arrangement, and flowers here, the *focal flowers*, are featured or emphasized by their location, size, and bold forms. They appear to be, and often actually are, the heaviest flowers in the arrangement, so focal flowers visually make sense when they rest at or near the bottom of the design, in keeping with the law of gravity. Focal flowers tend to be (but don't necessarily have to be) dark or intense colors, which are visually heavy. Progressively smaller, finer, lighter-looking materials are positioned upward and outward from the focal area.

An arrangement made to be viewed in the round may have a focal area, but the focal area is usually more obvious in an arrangement with a front and a back. Notice that three peonies are the focal flowers in the ikebana arrangement pictured on page 78. Look at and read about the focal flowers in the dried arrangement on page 84. In every case, the eye is drawn to these featured flowers, a phenomenon sometimes known as dominance.

Balance

In its literal application, balance in floral design means physical stability. In a well-balanced arrangement, the center of gravity is low, since heavy focal materials rest just above the rim of the vase, and the weight is evenly distributed and, if necessary, held in place with mechanics so the arrangement won't shift or topple. An arrangement with huge dahlia blossoms at the bottom and airy statice at the outer edges is balanced if all other components are also in balance. However, if the reverse is true and the dahlias tower over the statice, the arrangement is sure to be (and look) disturbingly top-heavy.

Most important aesthetically is that an arrangement not just be, but *look*, balanced. If it is symmetrical, so that the flowers and design on one side of the central axis mirror the other side, the arrangement is said to have formal visual balance.

Even if its physical shape is asymmetrical, an arrangement can still be balanced if the components are balanced visually (this is called informal balance). The concept of visual balance is analogous to the physical balance of a seesaw. In a symmetrical arrangement, balanced components on either side are the same distance from the fulcrum, or center point. But in an asymmetrical arrangement, a visually heavy focal flower far away from the fulcrum can stabilize several heavy focal flowers close to the fulcrum on the opposite side. For example, a red rose placed on the upper, outer portion of the arrangement may visually weigh as much as two or three red roses positioned on the other side of, and next to, the central axis.

A related principle is that one visually heavy element can balance a much larger quantity of visually light material. For example, a focal flower such as a gerbera, with its bold, solid form, situated close to the central axis may balance perfectly, and interestingly, with a diffuse mass of baby's breath at the opposite edge. When you consider that pale and bright colors are visually light, and dark colors visually heavy, as discussed in the section on color (see page 65), you can see the numerous ways in which the eye can be set into motion—and satisfied—by informal balance achieved though the use of both form and color. Every arrangement, traditional or contemporary, must have visual balance to be pleasing.

Proportion

Closely related to the balance of an arrangement are its proportions—the relationship between the size and mass of the plant materials and those of the container. In a perfectly proportioned floral design, the proportions aren't consciously noticed by most viewers. But when the proportions are incorrect, the arrangement appears ungainly and squat or top-heavy and precarious.

Rules for proportion have evolved for both ikebana and Western floral design. The length of the principal line in most Japanese arrangements is one and one-half times the width plus depth of the container. The next-longest line is three fourths of the length of the longest line, and the third is three fourths of the length of the second-longest line. The height of an arrangement in the Western tradition, from the bottom of the container to the highest point, is one and one-half to two times the height (or the width, if it is greater than the height) of the container.

Many pleasing arrangements can be designed without following these rules closely. If you are a beginner, however, you will find it helpful to incorporate them into your designs until you gain experience.

Rhythm

Anything that catches the eye and moves it in a given direction through an arrangement lends rhythm to the arrangement. The materials in a line arrangement, usually selected for their elegant curves, may produce slow, sinuous rhythms, gracefully contorted or abruptly zigzagging rhythms, or smooth, fast rhythms. Placing daffodils at exact intervals along the central axis or the outline may produce a monotonous rhythm, but irregular spacing or placement in twisting, spiraling, or angled lines can produce a pleasing rhythm.

Gradation of forms also creates an interesting rhythm, such as a progression from fully open daffodils at the center of an arrangement to half-open ones or tight buds at the edges. A rhythm is produced by the simple gradation of large hosta leaves to smaller ones. Moving from wide-open white anthuriums to cup-shaped white tulips to tightly furled white calla lilies creates a rhythm that resembles an opening flower spike, with a progression from the lower open flowers upwards to tight buds (see the arrangement on page 75).

Contrasts can create rhythms, too—for example, alternating solid with lacy forms toward the gradual dominance of one, or creating patterns of sharp-edged, flat forms interspersed among globular, ragged-edged, globular ones—hibiscus among alliums, for example.

When we think of flower arranging, we almost always think of the kind of organization implied in the earlier discussions of overall forms and forms within designs. But another possibility, long recognized in the Orient and adopted by European floral designers in this century, is beginning to influence American flower arranging.

Radial composition Most arrangements pictured in this book are radial compositions. Seen from above, the stems radiate outward like spokes; seen at eye level, they spread upward and outward from one point or area. Loose flowers placed in deep containers automatically fall into this pattern. Traditional European and American flower arrangements are radial. However, what if the container is shallow? Though pinholders and other mechanics still make radial composition possible, another possibility arises.

Parallel composition In arrangements that use parallel composition, the stems are positioned parallel to one another instead of radiating from a central point. The idea probably originated with a Japanese "natural scenery" style of arranging, which depicts a miniature landscape constructed in a shallow container. In these arrangements, plants of only one kind, or of various kinds, from trees to small flowers, are represented, though of course not

always to scale. As in a real landscape, the stems are all vertical or nearly vertical and are therefore parallel. European floral designers have devised a similar form of composition whose basic principles are that stems are parallel (but not necessarily vertical) and equally spaced. A parallel-style arrangement may group together all daffodils in one area, all forget-me-nots in another, and all fern fronds in another, or it may mix different kinds of flowers and foliage, or use only one kind of flower. On pages 90 and 91 a parallel arrangement is illustrated and discussed; on pages 76 and 77 you will see and read about an arrangement that combines aspects of both parallel and radial styles.

Color and Texture

The surface qualities of an arrangement are as important as its form. As we have already seen, surface and form can work together in many ways to create some of the strongest, most satisfying visual effects. Part of the challenge and much of the keenest pleasure in arranging flowers come from working with texture and color. Their use in floral design is highly personal and subjective, yet some basic principles govern the way the eye responds to them. Arrangers who are aware of those principles

Lily-of-the-valley stems converge at a central point within the vase, illustrating radial composition.

A wide-mouthed rectangular vase makes possible a parallel composition of narcissus without mechanics.

have at their disposal some of the most valuable resources in the art of flower arranging.

COLOR

To most people's eyes, color is the single most powerful element of floral design. Used effectively, color gratifies, soothes, astounds, or in other ways satisfies our eyes and our feelings. Used less effectively, it can be unappealing. Working with color to make an arrangement is in itself an adventure. When you work with color, experiment freely, but also let the following facts and ideas about color serve as shortcuts to help you achieve some pleasing effects and avoid some disappointing ones.

THE COLOR WHEEL AND COLOR HARMONY

The color wheel represents the whole color spectrum bent into a circle. It provides a convenient means of illustrating a number of useful facts about relationships between colors. The *primary colors* are blue, red, and yellow, and are equidistant on the wheel. All colors as you see them in this wheel are *hues* (pure colors), but in flowers and other natural materials you more often see *values* of these hues. An artist mixing paints can create values by adding white, black, or gray. Adding white to hues produces *tints*; adding black produces *shades*; and adding gray produces *tones*. As a flower arranger, you can achieve attractive and useful effects with colors if you understand the *harmonies* that exist between certain colors on the color wheel.

Monochromatic harmony is created by using tints, tones, and shades of one hue. The tulip arrangement on pages 82 and 83 uses a monochromatic color scheme. Because of the narrowness of color range, monochromatic color schemes tend to shift the emphasis away from color, toward form.

Analogous harmony is achieved by using a hue together with one to three of the colors adjacent to it on the color wheel. The best effects are often achieved when one color predominates rather than when all colors are used equally. The floating blossoms on page 12 are analogous colors, as are the flowers on the cover of this book.

Complementary harmony results when you combine two colors that directly oppose each other on the color wheel, such as yellow and violet. The contrast creates a powerful effect that is often best modulated by using values of one or both colors and by letting one color predominate.

Color, Size, and Space

A curious trick that color plays on the human eye is to create the illusion that warm-colored objects (red to yellow) are closer to the viewer than they really are, and that cool-colored objects (green to violet) are further away than they really are. You can use this principle to give an arrangement the appearance of depth. Place warm-colored flowers forward and cool-colored flowers and foliage deep within and toward the rear of the arrangement. Tints of these colors, since they have less visual weight, might be positioned high, and the heavier shades low.

The three color harmonies, illustrated from left to right, are monochromatic, adjacent, and complementary.

A related phenomenon is that cool and dark colors tend to get lost in a dimly lighted space. In a flower arrangement the result can be that all cool-colored or dark parts visually disappear in the dim light, leaving apparent voids. If you make an arrangement to be placed in a dimly lighted setting, use yellow, white, and bright red to fill spaces that otherwise might appear empty in the low light.

Bear in mind, too, that colors can make flowers seem larger or smaller than they really are. Dark colors seem to reduce size, and bright colors—yellow, white, and intense red—magnify size.

Psychological Effects of Color

Colors have definite effects on human emotion. Warm colors may be comforting to some personality types but agitating to others; cool colors may be either restful or depressing. Tints, including pastel colors, are thought to be cheery, and tones depressing. An arrangement with colors in

the green-to-violet range will probably make a stuffy July day seem less oppressive, and yellow-to-red flowers make a cool room cheerier on a bleak January afternoon.

So to an extent, correlations between colors and emotions can be pinpointed. But human response to color is very individual and subjective, so follow your own judgment and tastes as a flower arranger. Design with colors that are gratifying to your eye and seem appropriate for the setting or occasion.

TEXTURE

Texture has both tactile and visual qualities, reflected by the use of words such as rough, glossy, raspy, matte, satiny, waxy, ribbed, fuzzy, grainy, downy, and leathery. Every kind of flower and leaf has a texture and some plants have several textures. For example, a typical hosta leaf is both heavily ribbed and smooth, and the blossoms of an

Iceland poppy are both satiny and crinkly. Sharpening your awareness of texture opens up many possibilities when you arrange flowers and leaves.

Form, or Texture?

The distinction between form and texture can be a fine one. When forms are small or closely packed together, they create textures. This is because the forms cease to be perceived individually and instead are seen as a mass, or single form, with a particular texture. Each flower head of yarrow, fennel, hyacinth, and hydrangea, for example, is a form made of many tightly packed flowers that give it a distinctive texture. The asparagus fern in the arrangement on page 81 has a trailing contorted form, but its dominant feeling of soft airiness comes from the extremely delicate texture of the finely divided leaves. With massed plant materials of any scale, what is seen at close range as form becomes, at a distance, texture.

Contrasting Textures

The chief value of texture in floral design is the visual interest that it can produce through the use of contrast. Some interesting textural contrasts include: glossy, ribbed gardenia foliage and smooth, matte gardenia blossoms; shiny anthurium leaves among protea blossoms with their intricate, waxy filaments; pearly, parchmentlike dried seed capsules of money plant among fuzzy and feathery dried grasses and bristly artichoke thistle leaves. Study the textural contrasts in the foliage and flowers pictured on this page, in which the added dimension of color dramatically intensifies an already-strong visual appeal.

Texture and Color Together

The texture of a leaf or petal surface determines how intensely it reflects light. Surface reflection may be strong and direct, diffuse and muted, or somewhere between these extremes. A pink anthurium, with its glossy, flat surface, reflects enough light to be almost startlingly pink to the eye. A rose that is exactly the same shade of pink nevertheless appears softer in color because of its satiny rather than glossy surface. False spiraea of the same pink tint is softest and quietest of the three, because the fuzzy texture absorbs rather than reflects much of the light that strikes it. One practical application of this phenomenon might be to use smooth, glossy forms in a dimly lit spot, rather than fuzzy ones of the same shade, in order to project the color. Another technique is to use smooth textures in those places within an arrangement where you want the eye to rest.

Context

Every flower arrangement exists in the context of a place, a setting. It exists, as well, in the context of a particular time—a season, holiday, or other special occasion. Using flowers to celebrate seasons and occasions is discussed on pages 9 and 11.

A wide range of textures, from waxy and glossy to fine and prickly, are represented here.

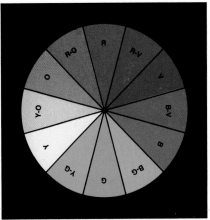

A color wheel is useful in studying relationships between colors.

As you set about making an arrangement, choosing the flowers and container and design, you'll have in mind a house that you know intimately, and a spot within it. Style of decoration as well as colors, textures, lighting, and vantage points will be so familiar that you will hardly need to check or ponder them, once you have made an arrangement or two for each spot.

A useful way to begin thinking about designing for a particular setting is to recognize that the flower arrangement is a part of a larger arrangement. It falls within the context of an entire room, a section of it, or a spot perhaps on a particular chest against a particular wall, just as a focal flower falls within the context of the entire flower arrangement. This means that the form, color, and texture of the container of flowers and of the setting are interrelated. Virtually every consideration that you give to matters of form, color, and texture within an arrangement applies on a larger scale to the arrangement within its setting.

As you design for this setting, you should give particular attention to scale, background, and style.

SCALE

The scale of an arrangement within its setting is analogous to the proportion of the flowers in relation to the vase that holds them. An arrangement that is too big for its setting is like a top-heavy mass of flowers in a small vase—awkward, and disturbing to the eye. An undersized arrangement can look lost in a large space unless it is skillfully situated to be a lovely detail in the overall scheme. If an arrangement neither crowds and overpowers nor creates a sense of barrenness, its scale is appropriate.

BACKGROUND

Always give careful consideration to the specific visual background for an arrangement. Which forms, colors, and textures would be harmonious and which would appear fussy (or would nearly disappear) against the figured wallpaper of your breakfast nook? What outline and colors would look best against the stark, well-lighted ecru wall of your dining room? What design could you use to great advantage in that difficult spot in front of the large mirror in the entryway? What flowers would look best viewed from above, at close range, beneath the lamp on the rosewood table at the bottom of the stairway? Solutions to these problems call for an understanding of many of the same basic design principles that you would employ within an arrangement. Here, however, the challenge in each case isn't simply to make a beautiful arrangement, but to make one whose beauty is appropriate to, and enhanced by, the background.

Remember the effects of dim lighting on certain colors if your arrangement will be displayed in low light (page 66). Light flowers for dark-colored backgrounds and dark flowers for light-colored backgrounds are usually safe choices. Too sharp a contrast, however, can distort or exaggerate forms in unflattering ways.

STYLE

The dried arrangement shown on page 84, with its multiplicity of colors and textures and its classical form, demands a traditional, somewhat formal setting. The exuberant country arrangement shown on page 76 calls for a relaxed, informal, even rustic setting in which the willow basket, the bountiful but carefully arranged flowers, and the unrestrained mixture of warm colors would be at home. The bold but simple tropical arrangement pictured on this page is perfectly suited to its contemporary interior—and it would look out of place if its free form and exotic materials were placed with period furniture and brocade draperies.

Depending on their materials and lines, many contemporary designs lend themselves to a wide range of interior styles. The tulip arrangement on pages 82 and 83, with its purity of form and color, could fit harmoniously into a very formal, traditional interior or a contemporary one, but it is too polished and its container too formal for a rustic setting. The elegant and open all-white arrangement in the simple glass vase (see page 75) is shown in a rustic setting. Yet, its cleanness of line and subtle color scheme suit it equally well to a contemporary interior. The airy bouquet shown on page 70, with its clear, spherical container and its overall simplicity, is stylistically neutral enough to fit into any interior. You can use a modest color scheme (maybe just one color), one, two, or three kinds of flowers, and a clean-lined, unobtrusive container to make an arrangement that will suit your home perfectly, whatever its style.

The dramatic tropical arrangement of dried bamboo with proteas, orchids, and flax leaf echoes the natural colors and fibers as well as the horizontal and diagonal lines of the spare, contemporary interior.

Containers

Containers are the "other half" of flower arrangements—as integral, if not as showy, as the flowers that they hold. Your possibilities in designing with flowers are governed in large measure by the array of containers at hand. As shown on this page, you can go well beyond conventional vases to find containers whose shapes, forms, colors, and textures suit a variety of design needs. Read on page 53 about practical considerations in selecting and using containers for fresh or dried cut flowers.

When you select a container, consider its style and degree of formality in relation to the setting, the occasion, and the plant materials that you will use. Always consider the size, color, shape, and texture of the container in relation to both context and flowers, using the basic design principles discussed in this chapter wherever you find them applicable and useful.

Generally you will use, at two extremes, rough-hewn or earthy containers such as wicker, crockery, terra-cotta, or galvanized tin to hold bright, rough-textured, irregularly shaped flowers for an informal country-style setting and, in a formal context, containers made of materials such as silver and crystal, and flowers with more refined forms, colors, and textures. A special consideration is the texture of a container, which, along with its style, shape, and color, determine its degree of formality. Usually a container works best when its texture corresponds to the prevailing texture of the flowers. Experiment with exceptions, however, like the garden roses in the antique galvanized tub (page 81).

Let simplicity be your guiding principle. The container should both complement the flowers and shift attention toward them, away from itself. One attractive use of clear glass containers is to display flower stems as a very visible and important part of the arrangement (as on page 75). Basic geometric shapes, minimal ornamentation or none at all, and subdued, neutral colors (black, white, and delicate or muted tints and shades) will prove most versatile and most pleasing to your eye.

This container collection only begins to illustrate the many shapes, colors, and materials available.

An informal arrangement requiring no mechanics features roses, freesia, stephanotis, dill, and other garden materials, including grasses.

A GALLERY
OF
ARRANGEMENTS

Each arrangement in this diverse series is accompanied by an analysis of its design, materials, and mechanics. Create similar arrangements tailored to your own taste, or use the concepts presented here as inspiration for your own unique designs.

The purpose of this concluding chapter is to offer you close-up views and detailed analyses of a gallery of diverse arrangements. Much that you have already learned is applied concretely here, through pictures and words. This chapter examines design concepts, flowers and other plant materials, containers, mechanics, procedures, appropriate settings for the arrangements, and ways to adapt the ideas in them to your own purposes.

Each arrangement has been included because it represents a distinct and important style, a popular kind of flower, or a special technique of arranging. Though you may not choose to copy any of them precisely, examining these arrangements will begin to reveal the vast range of possibilities open to you, and you will discover ideas to adapt to your tastes, your particular needs, and the materials at hand.

The photographs and text that follow might serve here and there as reminders that you can find inspiration for a successful floral design in any of myriad ways. One starting point for a design can be availability of flowers; a bounty of roses in the summer garden might have provided inspiration for the arrangement shown and discussed on pages 80 and 81; conversely, perhaps the designer of the arrangement on page 78 made a virtue of necessity after she found only three presentable blossoms in her small garden.

Some designers begin with a concept; a concept was the starting point for the arrangement discussed and illustrated on pages 74 and 75. Minimizing color and focusing on form and texture to create a floral sculpture might have been the designer's objective before she chose the materials or worked out the form. A special container is sometimes the designer's starting point—and the same floral sculpture could as easily have begun with the inspiring vase as with the idea of floral sculpture. For that matter, it could have begun with a particular spot, perhaps a bare table near a sunny window, that cried out for shimmering white flowers. One of the most common and best inspirations for a lovely design is the inherent nature of the flowers chosen by the designer. The purity and perfect forms of the tulips, in fact, had everything to do with the conception of the design pictured on pages 82 and 83, and the habits, texture, colors, and forms of the plants used inspired the arrangement on page 91.

So seize on whatever circumstance, perception, or impulse prompts you to begin thinking about making a particular flower arrangement. There are no rules for finding inspiration. Add to your fund of design inspirations the ideas and images that this gallery of arrangements provides. They will lead you to create some of your most satisfying arrangements.

Trumpet plant and a variegated bromeliad blend strikingly with more common flowers like nerine and delphinium.

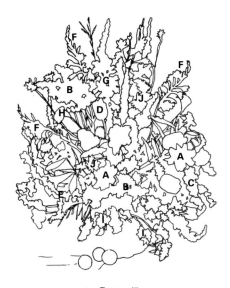

A Easter lily
B White lilac
C Purple lilac
D Tulip
E Hawthorn
F Watsonia
G Foxglove
H Calla
I Freesia
J Maple

An Old Masters Bouquet

Paintings by the Dutch and Flemish Old Masters (see page 6) inspired this sumptuous bouquet. Many arrangements made today are descendants of the mixed bouquets depicted in the Old Masters' floral still lifes. The Old Masters painted masses of flowers, but individual blossoms always remained distinct. The Old Masters look can be achieved with a modest number of short-to-medium stems of several varieties, or with an extravagant array that includes large-scale flowers.

Rather than paint actual arrangements of flowers gathered at one time, the Old Masters often combined flowers from several seasons in their paintings, to represent the bounty of a garden over much or all of the year. Modern horticultural methods enable you to arrange flowers that span seasons, like the flowers shown here. Instead, of course, you can make seasonal bouquets of flowers from your garden—or you can enrich your garden selection with florist flowers.

DESIGN AND FLOWERS

In this arrangement, white to pastel flowers, together with touches of deeper-colored lilac and hawthorn, make a large, sedate oval suitable for a sitting room in a formal, traditional interior. Notice how the flowers and foliage create strong visual interest with their contrasting textures. There are the large, smooth forms of tulips, callas, and Easter lilies; the smaller, cupped freesias and airy stems of watsonia with their smooth, graduated, tubular blossoms and buds, echoed by the graduated trumpets and close-set globular buds of foxglove; the crenulated, starlike maple leaves and smaller-scale hawthorn leaves; the wiry, elegant stems and blossoms of wild grass; and the dainty filigree of lilac and hawthorn. The overall effect is that of a floral tapestry.

To create a more casual bouquet for informal interiors, use flowers such as marguerite, cornflower, coreopsis, daylily, zinnia, money plant, stock, sunflower, love-in-a-mist, pincushion flower, coneflower, and roadside grasses and wildflowers. See the photograph on the title page of this book for an example of an Old Masters-–inspired bouquet with a casual feeling in which garden flowers, wildflowers, and grasses paint a radiant, relaxed picture of midsummer luxuriance. The bouquets on the cover of this book and page 70 have the Old Masters in their ancestry. Their simplicity, airiness, and soft colors suit them to a wide range of interior styles, from stark and contemporary to formal and traditional.

MATERIALS AND TECHNIQUES

Smaller bouquets in the Old Masters manner, particularly if the shapes of their containers and the bulk of their stems can hold flowers upright, may require no mechanics. However, for this imposing arrangement, the designer has filled the lined French wire basket with a brand of floral foam that holds flowers securely in place but is soft enough to be penetrated by tender stems. Sphagnum moss hides the floral foam and stem bases.

Once the designer settled on the color scheme and flowers, the procedure was straightforward. First he inserted the stems that define height, width, and overall shape. Then he began filling out the design, with the largest flowers concentrated at and just below medium height, the larger spikes tapering toward the upper edges, and the smaller and curving spikes placed mainly at the middle and lower edges. By extending the floral foam above the rim of the container, he was able to angle some outer stems downward so they trail gracefully over its edge, adding to the soft fullness of the design and defining the bottom of the oval.

The designer cut stems to lengths that fit his design. Here some watsonia, tulip, and calla stems have been slightly shortened, and lily and foxglove stems have been severely cut, yet never so much that any of the flowers look squat and unnatural. The side facing the nearby wall has no detail, but the arrangement could easily be rounded out if it were intended to be seen from all sides.

Of the myriad possibilities in floral design, a large, Old Masters–inspired bouquet like this one is perhaps the richest and most opulent of arrangements. This style can be adapted to a range of related designs, large and elaborate or small and simple, formal or informal. In a smaller, more casual form, such a design could still be a celebration of spring—or summer, or fall—showing off seasonal flowers. The style blends with Oriental carpets, rich fabrics, and period furnishings. It contrasts effectively with spare but handsomely detailed interiors. You might use it to emphasize richness of decor, or to unify several colors in an interior.

A Sculptural All-White Design

By eliminating all color except for the subtlest shades of near white, the designer of this sophisticated arrangement has created an arresting study in form and texture.

DESIGN AND FLOWERS

At first glance, this arrangement appears to contain uniformly white flowers. Closer inspection, however, reveals its delicate coloration. Its materials are not simply stark white but include spikes of chincherinchee with greens that gradually dissolve into white or near-white. In addition, there are creamy to yellow-white anthuriums and callas and creamy tulip blossoms. All of these near whites contrast with the deep to medium green foliage and stems. Thus, one dimension of this fascinating design is its subtle use of color.

Because color is minimal, the elegant, varied forms and textures of blossoms and leaves stand out. The heavily veined, heart-shaped anthurium flowers seem to have been carved from wax. Like the anthuriums, the callas taper to points, but they are furled funnels and their surface texture is matte. Midway between these textural extremes are the tulips, whose oval and chalice shapes are also intermediate between the tight funnels and open, flat hearts of the callas and anthuriums. The chincherinchees, like the anthuriums and callas, taper to a point; their overall form, however, is not a curved surface but an aggregate of small stars and smaller oval buds couched among fine green filaments. All stems—prominent elements in the design—are straight or gently arched. Narrow, finely tapered tulip leaves curve languidly over the edge of the base. The two anthurium leaves, related in form to the anthurium blossoms, hover like two stylized clouds in an old Chinese painting or two sections of a contemporary mobile.

The overall form of the arrangement is a loose V shape. Its right prong, though containing fewer stems than the left one, is given equalizing visual weight by the anthurium leaf. This leaf is larger than the leaf on the other side, and its dark, heavy mass extends farther away from the central axis (see page 62).

Thus, while the textures and individual forms of the design lend it sculptural qualities here and there, it is particularly the ways in which the forms are combined that make a sculpture of the whole arrangement.

MATERIALS AND TECHNIQUES

The simple, asymmetric glass vase designed by Alvar Aalto provides an unobtrusive but elegant base for this floral sculpture. The use of clear glass keeps in full view the stems and mechanics, which are elements of the overall design. Because the designer selected the large, open vase for rather few stems, she devised natural-looking mechanics that blend with the living materials. Corkscrew willow wound about inside the bottom of the vase accentuates its asymmetry and forms a network of holes to support stems; floral wire wrapped in green tape spirals around the anthurium stems and loops to form brackets that hold the leaves horizontal; raffia binds the three branches of calla stems, which are far easier to control when grouped than when inserted separately. Each bunch of callas is terraced—trimmed and arranged so that the blossoms are gracefully staggered.

The designer began by first placing the corkscrew willow mechanics, then grouping, tying, and inserting the callas. Next, she inserted the chincherinchees, and finally, she added the thin-stemmed anthurium flowers and leaves. Since the anthurium leaves strike the final balance, it was logical to save them for last.

To make an arrangement whose sculptural quality is the key idea in the design,

use white or monochromatic, pale flowers. Such flowers as rose, Madagascar jasmine, zinnia, tuberose, poppy, daffodil, nicotiana, orchid (perhaps *Phalaenopsis*), magnolia, lily, amaryllis, hyacinth, freesia, and foxtail lily can be used in striking combinations to create sculptural effects. Experiment freely, with an eye to creating pleasing combinations of textures and forms. Consider grouping individual blossoms of one kind to build larger, bolder units, as this designer has done with callas. Avoid a cluttered, fussy look.

Its simplicity allows this design to look perfectly at home in a rustic, early American setting—but it would also be in its element in a Bauhaus or contemporary interior. Even in a white Victorian bedroom it would harmonize with the decor. Whatever the interior style, a sunny (but not too hot) window setting will make it shimmer. And as warmth encourages the flowers to develop—the callas to unfurl, and tulips and chincherinchees to open, turn, and grow taller—this design will be an ever-changing sculpture.

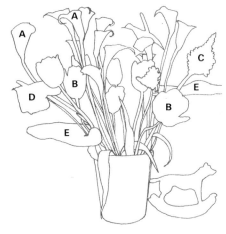

A Calla lily
B Tulip
C Chincherinchee
D Anthurium
E Anthurium leaf

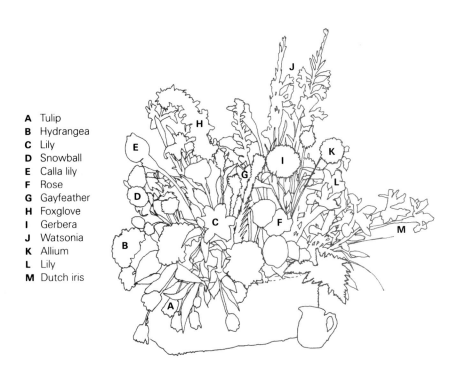

A Tulip
B Hydrangea
C Lily
D Snowball
E Calla lily
F Rose
G Gayfeather
H Foxglove
I Gerbera
J Watsonia
K Allium
L Lily
M Dutch iris

Country Flowers With a Continental Touch

Exuberant late-spring and early-summer flowers fill and spill over the edges of this country basket. The arrangement reflects the designer's familiarity with two concepts, one old and the other new, which she has deftly combined to achieve this simple, spontaneous look in a design that can be viewed from any angle.

DESIGN AND FLOWERS

This arrangement borrows from the large-scale European mixed bouquet, with Old Masters paintings and traditional English and French country-style designs in its background. Abundant garden flowers have been mixed to create a floral cornucopia. A broad range of both soft and brilliant colors underlines the casual, profuse style of this bouquet. Some repetition of color among varieties, such as the pink repeated among the tulips, hydrangeas, watsonias, and alliums, unifies the bold mixture.

The design of this country basket arrangement also borrows from parallelism, the concept of grouping flowers along a horizontal plane. The pink tulips and yellow Dutch irises have been grouped to spread outward from their respective points along this plane, much as they would grow from their spots in a mixed garden border. Yet here they have been trimmed, angled, and arranged into an artful form. Closer scrutiny reveals that the other flowers have been similarly grouped and blended into the overall design. To enhance the naturalistic effect as well as to fill in and soften the line between basket and flowers, foliage has been added low in the arrangement.

MATERIALS AND TECHNIQUES

The bleached willow basket helps to establish the casual country feeling. Like the flowers, it is light and romantic in spirit. Its long, rectangular shape allows space for the many groupings of flowers. Inside the basket, floral foam in a plastic liner holds the stems in place.

The designer's procedure was first to place at least one stem of every grouping, including the longest stems of the arrangement, to establish the locations of groupings as well as the outline of the design. Then she filled in the groupings, moving freely around the whole arrangement as she worked. Special care was given to angling the tulips downward and the Dutch irises into upward- and outward-reaching forms. She added hydrangea, fern, and salal foliage last.

To make your own mixed country bouquet with groupings of flowers, pick your color scheme and, unless your arrangement needs to last only a day or so, be careful to select flowers with similar vase lives (see the charts on pages 22 to 37). Use foliage where needed to fill in, to set off flowers, and to soften the line between container and flower as the leather fern and tulip leaves do here. Let groupings overlap as they might in the garden. Look for a rustic container appropriate for country flowers, though not necessarily oblong or rectangular. Some suitable containers include a low, wide crockery urn, a copper or brass pot or kettle, a fruit basket, a weathered produce or firewood box, a painted or natural wicker basket, an enameled roaster, or a small galvanized tub.

This ample basket would look best in a traditional interior, informal or even rustic in feeling. On an entryway table or chest it would be cheery and welcoming. On a sideboard or a buffet it could bring pleasure to diners. Its generous proportions suit it better to a large room or an open hallway than to a small, intimate room. Wherever it is used, the casualness and affluence of a seasonal border in a country garden spills over into the house.

Ikebana:
Two Examples of Simple Elegance

These two radiant examples of *ikebana*—the Japanese art of flower arranging—are as spare and apparently simple as the Old Masters arrangement on page 72 is lush and elaborate. Their precise yet spontaneous-looking designs are based on concepts that have evolved over centuries of Japanese history, with Chinese and Korean origins. Symbolism and nuances of meaning are evident only to the eye trained to read them. However, understanding these esoteric ideas is entirely unnecessary for you to make similar arrangements. All you need are a few easy instructions, a love of flowers, and—if only for a few minutes—quiet and peace of mind. The arrangements shown here should not be viewed merely as examples of designs suitable for beginners; many accomplished ikebana practitioners, after they have mastered more elaborate forms, return frequently to the satisfying simplicity of designs such as these.

DESIGN AND FLOWERS

Each of these arrangements contains only two kinds of plant materials: Peruvian daffodils and rushes in one (see opposite page), forsythia branches and peonies in the other (see this page). Forsythia and peony are popular garden plants, and Peruvian daffodils thrive in gardens in moderate to mild climates. Rushes are seldom marketed but abound in marshy spots over much of the country. Even if you purchased all of the materials, these arrangements would be as inexpensive as their designs are simple.

You can just as effectively use any flower close to these in size to make similar arrangements. For example, instead of peonies, substitute roses, marigolds, proteas, ranunculus, poppies, lilies, carnations, dogwood, dahlias, tulips, or ornamental onions. For Peruvian daffodils, substitute common daffodils (*Narcissus*), columbines, coreopsis, purple coneflowers, sea holly, love-in-a-

mist, pincushion flowers, or nasturtiums. Many kinds of foliage will serve as well as forsythia. The rushes used here are but one of many common species that you might use, or you might substitute any of a multitude of wild grasses to create similar effects.

The arrangement in the low, black ceramic container is in the very popular *moribana* style, whose name means "piling up of flowers." Moribana arrangements are always done in low containers; black is unobtrusive in most settings and directs

attention to the plant materials themselves. This arrangement has three primary stems that represent the three traditional major elements in ikebana design: The longest upright stem represents heaven; the next-highest point of emphasis, here the sharp-angled stem left of the central axis, represents man; and the lowest stem, the sharp-angled one on the right, underlying the other two elements, represents earth. Shape is strongly geometric, in this case an overlapping series of stark triangles frames the soft fullness of the blossoms. The focal point, to which the eye moves first, is just above the central edge of the vase, where all stems converge; here the lowest three blossoms define it. (Notice that in this and other Japanese arrangements, elements appear in threes or multiples of three.)

The other arrangement is in the *nageire*, sometimes termed *heika* ("tall vase") style. This one is a "slanting design," so named for obvious reasons. Nageire means "thrown-in flowers," referring to the natural, rather than contrived, effect of this style, which suggests the informal lines of plants growing in a natural setting. The longest forsythia stem, arching to the left, represents heaven; the central stem, man; and the pendulous stem, earth. The peonies establish the focal point.

MATERIALS AND TECHNIQUES

Their extreme simplicity extends beyond design to the construction of these two arrangements. In the taller arrangement, in the nageire style, the shape of the vase and its small opening preclude the need for mechanics. In the vase used for the shorter arrangement, in the moribana style, a pinholder secures the plant materials. If the vase were wider, the pinholder would probably be camouflaged with pebbles like those on the table.

To make the moribana arrangement, the designer first inserted the tallest rush, establishing the "heaven" line; then she inserted and bent to the left the rush that forms the "man" line; and then she inserted and bent the "earth" rush, on the lower right. She next added the other, secondary, rushes, which contribute fullness and visual interest; and last she inserted the Peruvian daffodils, with the greatest concentration of them just at the rim of the vase.

To make the nageire arrangement, she followed a similar procedure, inserting "heaven," "man," and "earth" stems ("earth" is the lowest), then some secondary, leafy forsythia stems, and finally the focal peonies. Though when viewed from this angle, two of the peonies appear to touch, in fact none of them touch any of the others.

Both arrangements are made in strict accordance with the rules of their styles. Though they are Japanese, their utter simplicity suits them to a wide range of interiors, including virtually all contemporary ones. The moribana arrangement, with its obviously Japanese vase and dramatic angles, might seem out of place in a rustic or a formal period interior. The nageire arrangement suggests a contemporary setting. However, because it is so neutral in its container and lines, it would suit any but a very rustic interior.

Unless you wish to, there is no reason to adhere strictly to the rules of ikebana. Certainly there is much to be learned from the simplicity and gracefulness of ikebana that you can apply to your own designs. Each of the arrangements pictured here demonstrates that an arrestingly elegant design can be created with a bare handful of materials, and that the humblest materials often serve at least as well as the costliest.

A Profusion of Favorites

Some flowers more than others embody the singular magic of their season in the garden. An extravagance that you can probably manage at least once a season, particularly if you have a productive cutting garden, is a large container overflowing with one of these seasonal specialties. A mixed bouquet has its charms and pleasures, but a mass of a single kind of flower, especially one of the great favorites, is incomparable. When you make such an arrangement, much of the satisfaction comes from finding a design that shows the flowers to their best advantage and emphasizes the qualities that make them stars of the seasonal garden.

SUMMER ROSES

Nothing could be more sumptuous or indulgent to the senses than a big bouquet of mixed, summer garden roses. Wherever they are placed, their heady fragrance and soft colors cast a spell of summertime languor. This bouquet enhances the coziness of a bedroom, but it would be as appropriate in a sitting room, dining room, or entryway with a traditional decor.

Something different from the usual vase, something quietly dramatic, something to play up the softness of the roses; these objectives led the designer to choose the antique galvanized tub as the container for this arrangement. A note of spontaneity and casualness is also introduced by the tub, in which the roses appear to have been brought directly from the garden. The tub's flat, gray patina provides a perfect foil for the satiny blossoms of lavender-pink, deep rose, fleshy pink, and cream.

If you want to achieve a more formal, upscale effect with a mass of roses, you might use a crystal, glass, or silver container—and you might use one variety only (and therefore a single color). The designer's purpose here, however, was to keep the mood informal and to get as far as possible away from the cliché of long-stemmed red roses in a crystal vase.

A large block of standard floral foam, whose sphagnum-covered top rises several inches above the rim of the tub, holds the roses just where the designer wants them. Because many of the stems are short, it serves not only to support the stems, but also to boost the blossoms to desired heights. The foam also makes it possible to angle one or two roses, along with some of the asparagus fern, outward and downward, to enhance the feeling of softness and languor.

The designer started by positioning the trailing wisps of asparagus fern and the few long, angled rose stems. Then he inserted the bulk of the roses, working both to distribute colors, with darker, heavier tones mainly toward the bottom, and to display buds and blossoms at various stages of development throughout the bouquet. He added a few more stems of asparagus fern to accentuate the softness of the roses—and softness, after all, is the key concept in the design of this romantic bouquet.

SPRING TULIPS

Just as the bouquet in the tub captures the romantic essence of summer garden roses, this big bouquet (see pages 82 and 83) suggests the pristine purity of spring tulips, and of spring itself. It contains only tulips, both blossoms and foliage, and everything—tulips, container, and accessories—contributes to the feeling of purity.

The French silver bowl is elegantly chaste: gracefully curved and simply worked at its edges, and as symmetrical as the overall arrangement itself. No color, fussy ornamentation, or startling shape distracts the eye from the tulips; instead, the simplicity of the bowl complements them. Subtle flower tints in a narrow color range—creamy white to delicate pink—suggest simplicity and purity. The nearly colorless blossoms strike the eye as pure forms rather than patches of color. The tight, perfect ovals, chalice shapes, and slightly ruffled forms of the peony tulips are accentuated by the soft green of the leaves.

For this arrangement the designer chose a special floral foam for tender stems. Into it, around the longer edges of the oval-shaped container, he first inserted the gracefully nodding stems; they had wilted during their shipment from Holland and were revived but retained their curves because he purposely kept them unwrapped during conditioning.

Then he added the remainder of the tulips, building the design upward to form the full, horizontal oval.

The nearly neutral color scheme and the symmetry of this large arrangement lend it versatility, making it perfectly suited to a formal, traditional setting or a contemporary one enriched by old rugs and a few simple-lined antiques. In a less elegant container, the character of the design would be altered. A stark, ceramic container such as a soufflé dish would make it compatible with even the most austere contemporary interior. A plain, earthy container would adapt it to a rustic setting.

You can use tulips to create an arrangement similar to this one, or you may use them quite differently, but with equal success, to make a mass display. Consider, for example, the various moods that you could create by using any one of the many colors of tulips, or by mixing colors. However you design with tulips, bear in mind that in the vase they continue to grow and change. Their stems elongate and reorient themselves as the blooms reach toward light sources, and the blossoms open wider. The original effect may alter, but much of the pleasure of living with cut tulips is in their kinetic nature.

A 'Sweet Surrender'
B 'French Lace'
C 'Heirloom'
D 'Lavonne'

Overleaf: A bouquet of spring tulips.

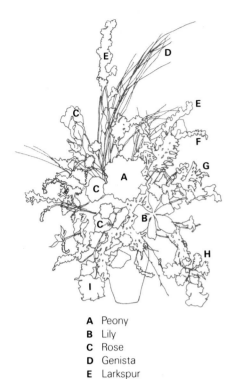

A Peony
B Lily
C Rose
D Genista
E Larkspur
F Lavender
G Statice
H Oak
I Maple

An Elegant Dried Arrangement

Unlike a typical country-rustic arrangement of dried weeds, grasses, or garden flowers in a basket, this arrangement of dried flowers has been designed to harmonize with the quiet formality of a study in a traditionally decorated house. The clear colors, smooth petals, and distinct forms of most of the focal blossoms add just the right degree of polish needed to make dried flowers succeed elegantly in a style usually reserved for fresh flowers. The designer found her inspiration in several canvases by Jan van Huysum, one of the most celebrated of the Old Masters painters.

DESIGN AND FLOWERS

The vertical, glossy black vase, with its classical lines, both helps to establish the formal tone and holds the flowers high

enough that some blossoms, branches, and foliage can flow down over its edge. This spilling effect echoes the sense of bountifulness often seen in van Huysum's floral still lifes. There is typical Old Masters variety, yet enough repetition of materials and colors to unify the design. Scarlet to faded red roses on the left balance the red berries on the other side of the central axis; the green stems of genista are repeated throughout; the blues and near-blues of larkspur are echoed in the lavender and statice; and the yellow to buff tones are shared by the maple leaves, sunflowers, the uppermost rose, the lily, and the peony.

The focal peony, with its attractively crumpled texture and its parchment tones, is obviously dried, yet is bright and showy. It ties together the brighter, fresher-looking focal flowers (the lily, the lower roses, and the sunflowers) and the duller, dried-looking line and filler materials. Among the flowers used as filler are lavender, statice, berries, and the smaller individual blossoms. Materials extend outward to round the arrangement, which is designed to be viewed from three sides.

You can use any combination of compatible-looking dried flowers and other dried plant materials to achieve much the same effect. In such a dried arrangement, the focal flowers are featured even more emphatically than those in a typical fresh arrangement of the same style, so choose and prepare them with special care.

This arrangement is particularly suited to a period interior—Tudor or Georgian, for example. It would not fit an extremely rustic setting or an austere contemporary one. In a study or library, it would be appropriate for a table in a small entryway or a chest or table in a sitting room.

MATERIALS AND TECHNIQUES

Most of the focal flowers—the lower roses and the lily—as well as the miniature carnations were preserved by the micro-

wave-silica gel method (see page 50). Everything else was air-dried; the oak and maple stems were set upright to dry. Because the lichen-covered oak was gathered in extremely hot, dry weather, it dried so rapidly that the leaves retained their greenness.

The designer chose a floral foam made for arranging dried flowers. In order to make the best use of the foam, and to anchor it firmly, she cut a small brick of foam, stood it upright, and after carefully measuring the neck of the vase, cut away two pieces of foam so that a T-shaped piece remained. The stem of the T slipped precisely and snugly into the vase. Then, with her knife, she rounded off the angular edges of the cap of the T, covered it with Spanish moss, and secured the moss to the foam with U-shaped, hairpin-like staples fashioned out of wire. At this point she was ready to begin her design.

First she positioned larkspur, genista, and the lower stem of oak (wired to extend its length) to establish the central axis and the outline. She then added the focal flowers, the maple leaves, and lastly the fine filler materials. Ordinarily in a dried arrangement, filler would be inserted before the focal flowers, because it is usually plentiful and easily supplemented or replaced if broken. Focal flowers, which are larger and more painstakingly preserved than the filler, might be crushed when filler is added. Here, however, the filler consists of numerous slender stems of assorted flowers whose insertion posed no threat to the already-positioned focal flowers.

If you make an arrangement similar to this one, consider adding accessories, like the persimmons and pomegranates here, to enlarge the feeling of bountifulness (and to expand the arrangement itself), to add further dimension to the still-life effect, and to enhance the colors of the flowers.

A Hand-Tied Bouquet: The Gracious European Gesture

This hand-tied bouquet represents the popular European practice of taking flowers to a hostess or to a friend one hasn't visited for a while. So called because it is held in the hand as it is arranged and bound securely together, the hand-tied bouquet requires only that the fortunate recipient drop it into a vase and enjoy it.

DESIGN AND FLOWERS

Pictured here is a hand-tied bouquet of summer flowers that has a contemporary feeling for several reasons: its overall simplicity; its free-form airiness created by the starkly elegant bear grass and horsetail and the sparsely leaved, angular birch stems; its bold, unconventional use of the subtly tinted green forms of allium and kalanchoe; and its generously spaced geometric shapes—textured globes, jointed blunt tubes, flaring funnels, filaments, serrated ovals, and overlapping flat circles.

As the casual, spontaneous look in flowers has become more popular, hand-tied bouquets have come to be used increasingly as wedding flowers. If you are planning flowers for a wedding, consider using hand-tied bouquets for bridal and bridesmaids' bouquets.

MATERIALS AND TECHNIQUES

In building this arrangement, the designer added one type of flower at a time to the bouquet, beginning with the horsetails and followed next by the birch stems. She then added the tall, heavy-stemmed flowers, the lilies. After she had added the chincherinchee, kalanchoes, cornflowers, and physostegias to build an easy-to-handle mass of stems, she added the slippery-stemmed alliums. On the outside of the bundle of stems she then inserted a few fine strands of bear grass to soften the design. Last, she added galax leaves to form a collar around the bouquet. The collar makes the arrangement easier to carry and helps to support it in the vase. The arranging completed, she bound the stems as described below and then cut them to approximately the same length, so that all could reach well into the water of the vase.

Some practice is often needed before you can hold flowers securely in one hand while you add to and adjust them with the other. A period of practice pays off, however, when you have gained the exceptional control of materials that this method permits. The ability to position flowers deftly and precisely is a decided advantage over other methods of arranging.

Once you've laid out your flowers and other plant materials within easy reach, the procedure for making a hand-tied bouquet is straightforward. The real key to success is to begin with stems whose texture makes them easy to grasp, rather than with long, smooth stems that slip easily..

As you work, cradle the stems firmly with your fingers and palm, but avoid crushing soft stems and mashing blossoms together. Use the thumb and carefully flex the palm and fingers to open and close around the stems. It is helpful to have someone on hand to tie the completed arrangement while you hold it, but practice will make you more and more adept at tying without letting stems slip. Wind the ribbon up and down around a wide band of the stem bundle, covering perhaps two or three inches. Then, work the ribbon between the bases of some of the substantial stems and pull it up to the wrapped band of stem, loop it again around the stems, and tie it. Cut the stems to about the length of the shortest stem. Until you present the bouquet, of course, you should keep its stems in water. You may also want to add decorative streamers, as shown here.

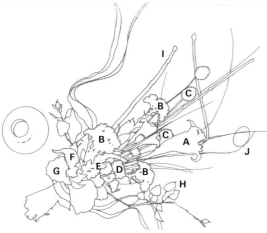

A Belladonna lily
B Kalanchoe
C Allium
D Cornflower
E Physostegia
F Chincherinchee
G Galax
H Birch
I Horsetail
J Bear grass

A Cheery Cluster Bouquet

A loose, casual cluster of small containers, each holding one stem of freesia, brightens this dinner table and brings to it both color and fragrance. This flexible arrangement of containers invites the diners to handle them—pick them up to smell the flowers, and move them around the table. The floral cluster is an active element in the shared enjoyment of an evening.

DESIGN AND FLOWERS

A handful of flowers and several small, flask-like vases create a big effect. Each stem is a gracefully arching spike with forms that gradually decrease in size, from open blossoms to smaller and greener buds. On a larger scale the cluster has the effect of a single, attractively diffuse bouquet. Soft, pastel colors are in keeping with the cool colors and clean surfaces of the wall, table, and place settings, and with the soft neutrality of the picture.

MATERIALS AND TECHNIQUES

The tubular necks and narrow mouths of the containers hold stems upright. To make cluster arrangements you can use almost any small, upright containers—for example, antique medicine vials, perfume bottles, or bud vases.

You can use a cluster any place in your home where flowers can be viewed at close range—such as on side tables, bedside chests, or low shelves. Stems of any kind of flower gain from being featured in individual containers. Use more than one variety to create the effect of a mixed bouquet. Individual blossoms or several stems of such flowers as peony, poppy, iris, lily, cosmos, and many types of orchid are among the numerous suitable subjects.

A Landscape Parallel

An important contemporary concept beginning to influence American floral design is applied here in a very individual manner with a rich array of plant materials from a garden in the western United States. The designer's purpose is, through materials and design, to create an impressionistic reflection of the garden.

DESIGN AND FLOWERS

The plant materials—to say "flowers" would be insufficient because there are fruits, berries, vegetables, and even withered sheaths, as well as leaves and flowers—suggest a bountiful garden in an arid climate. Edible as well as ornamental dry-climate and "oasis" plants flourish in this garden. A native penstemon and desert bromeliad, along with figs, red-hot pokers, prickly-pear fruits, and mandarin oranges are typical plants grown in the dry, hot-summer West. Components such as fuchsia, nasturtium, and rose hips hint at a moist "oasis" within the garden, as do berries, eggplant, and peppers. Plants in various stages of development, from budding and blooming to fruiting and withering, are represented just as they might appear in the midsummer garden.

The design embodies the principle of parallelism (see page 64). Instead of radiating outward from a hub, stems in a parallel composition are arranged as they grow from the ground, more or less parallel to one another. Plants of the same kind are grouped together naturalistically, as though growing from a common rootstock.

The warm, tawny color scheme uses values and shades of analogous colors. The red segment of the spectrum, from deep reddish purples through various reds to red-oranges and golds, conveys a sense of summer in the Southwest. Greens function neutrally as foils for the reds.

Use any color composition in a parallel design—but bear in mind that if your arrangement is intricate and finely de-

A Fuchsia
B Wild blackberry
C Desert penstemon
D Grevillea
E Nasturtium
F Bead plant
G Quince
H Coleus
I Red salvia
J Arum berries
K Arum (dried leaf sheath)
L Red-hot poker
M Red pepper
N Prickly pear cactus fruit
O Fig
P Mandarin orange
Q Eggplant

tailed, as this one is, your use of many colors widely separated in the spectrum can result in a cluttered, fussy effect that detracts from forms and textures.

MATERIALS AND TECHNIQUES

The container, like its contents, is a vegetative part of the garden. The designer cut a section from a large, dried agave stalk,

then split it in two and hollowed one half to hold a plastic liner. She then taped a long bar of floral foam into it.

After she had gathered her materials, she covered the ends of the container with vegetation, then inserted the taller stems, then the lower materials toward the middle. Most stemmed materials were inserted directly into the floral foam. Heavier or short-stemmed pieces—the quince and other fruits and vegetables—were either wired

onto the arrangement or anchored directly into the foam with wooden picks.

Parallelism offers a wealth of possibilities, from earthy and complex designs to ones that are stark, simple, and geometric. You can suggest a landscape not just by grouping several kinds of plants, but by juxtaposing groupings as they would actually appear in the garden or wild landscape For example, if ferns, violets, and horsetails grow together in the wild, they might make a grouping in your arrangement, and daisies, phlox, and meadow grass another one.

Or if you like the combination of bearded iris, delphinium, hosta foliage, and pincushion flower in a garden bed, you might combine them in a parallel arrangement. You can also make an entirely different application of parallelism—for example, using a cluster of flat glass vases for groupings of very vertical seasonal flowers such as allium, false spiraea, watsonia, and lily in combination with some round, soft, or sprawling forms such as fleabane, clematis, and statice.

The intricate naturalistic arrangement pictured here invites close inspection and contemplation. Its detailing and low mass make it a perfect centerpiece that would blend with contemporary or Mediterranean decor and bring to the dining table both beauty and a subject for conversation. It could also be viewed at close range against a light-toned sitting-room wall. Unlike many less complex arrangements, it gains rather than loses in interest after careful scrutiny, making it a work of art rather than simply an ornament.

A Single Blossom

Arrangements—combinations of flowers, or of flowers and other plant materials, within containers—have been considered throughout this book, and most concretely in this concluding chapter. The very term *arrangement* implies a multiplicity of things to be set into some sort of meaningful order. But one blossom in a simple container can make perhaps the most concentrated statement of floral beauty. A single blossom focuses the eye on the unity and completeness of one of nature's loveliest creations.

A carefully chosen blossom that harmonizes with its container and setting makes an intimate arrangement for viewing at close range. It also reminds us that when we arrange a mass of flowers we should never lose sight of the importance of individual blossoms, which are the basic units of the design. Even the most ordinary blossom—a daisy or a daffodil, for example—reveals its perfection when positioned in an arrangement so that it can be looked at closely.

Isolated from other blossoms, this torch cactus flower invites the eye to savor its beauty, and the mind to contemplate the phenomenon that this book has set out to explore: the wonderfully mysterious appeal of flowers.

Index

A

Acanthus (Bear's breech), 22–23
Acer (Maple), 11
  A. palmatum (Japanese maple), 22–23, 47
  in Old Masters bouquet, *72, 73*
  in Old Masters dried arrangement, *84,* 85
Achillea (Yarrow), 22–23
  in dried arrangement, 51
  drying, 49
  form and texture, 66
Additives, 44, 46, 47
Agapanthus (Lily-of-the-Nile, African lily), *22,* 22–23, *56, 58*
Agave stalk, as container, 90
Air-drying, 49
  gathering for, 48
  for Old Masters dried arrangement, 85
Alcea (Hollyhock), *22,* 22–23, 44
Allium (Allium, Ornamental onion), 7, *8,* 22–23
  in country-style arrangement, *76,* 77
  in hand-tied bouquet, 86, *86–87*
  for ikebana, 78
  for parallel cluster, 91
  rhythm with, 64
Almond, forcing, 47
Alstroemeria (Peruvian lily), 22–23
Amaryllis. *See Hippeastrum*
Analogous harmony, 65, *66*
  in landscape arrangement, 90–91, *90–91*
Anemone coronaria (Windflower), *5,* 22–23
  microwave drying, 51
  seed heads, *62*
Annual delphinium. *See Consolida*
Anthurium (Anthurium, Flamingo flower, Painted tongue), 22–23
  in all-white floral sculpture, 74, *75*
  buying from florists, 21
  light and texture, 67
  rhythm with, 64
Antirrhinum (Snapdragon), 22–23
Apple (*Malus*), 9, 32–33, 47
Appropriateness, 7, 9
  See also Setting
  containers, 69
  found materials, 38
Aquilegia (Columbine), 22–23, 78

Arrangement, defined, 7, 9, 92
Artichoke thistle, 67
Arum, 90–91, *90–91*
Asparagus fern, 66, 80, *80–81*
Aspirin, 46
Aster (Aster, Michaelmas daisy), 11, 22–23, 43
Aster, China. *See Callistephus*
Aster, Stokes'. *See Stokesia*
Astilbe (False spiraea, Meadowsweet), 22–23, *62*
  light and texture, 67
  for parallel cluster, 91
Autumn arrangements, 10, 11

B

Baby's breath. *See Gypsophila*
Baby shower bouquet, 12
Bachelor's button. *See Centaurea cyanus*
Background considerations, 68
Balance, 63
Bamboo, *68*
Basket arrangements, 12, *17,* 53
Bathroom arrangements, 7, *8*
Bead plant, 90–91, *90–91*
Bear grass, 86, *86–87*
Bear's breech. *See Acanthus*
Bearded iris. *See Iris*
Bedroom arrangements, 16
Begonia, *12*
Belladonna lily, *86–87*
Bellflower. *See Campanula*
Bells of Ireland. *See Moluccella*
Berries
  in autumn arrangements, 11
  in dried arrangement, *84,* 85
  as filler, 63
  glycerinating, 52–53
  in landscape arrangement, 90–91, *90–91*
  in winter arrangements, 9, 11
Betula (Birch), 86, *86–87*
Bird-of-paradise. *See Strelitzia*
Birthday arrangements, 12
Blackberry, 90–91, *90–91*
Blanket flower. *See Gaillardia*
Blazing star. *See Liatris*
Bleach
  in forcing water, 47
  in glycerine solution, 53
  in vase water, 46

Bluebell (*Scilla*), 36–37
Borax, as dessicant, 50
Botanical names, 21, 39
Bottle brush, *52,* 53
Bouquets, 7, 57
  cluster, *88–89,* 89
  country-style, *76,* 77
  hand-tied, 86, *86–87*
  as mass arrangements, 60
  Old Masters style, *6, 7, 72, 73, 84,* 85
  setting for. *See* Setting
  spring tulips, 80–81, *82–83*
  summer roses, 80, *80–81*
Boutonnieres, 56, *56*
Branches
  in autumn arrangements, 11
  forcing, 46–47
  in winter arrangement, 9
British floral design, 7
Bromeliads, *71*
  in Christmas arrangement, *11*
  in landscape arrangement, 90–91, *90–91*
Bud clusters, as filler, 63
Bulbs, 9
Butterfly flower. *See Schizanthus*

C

Calendula (Pot marigold), 22–23, 43
Calla lily. *See Zantedeschia*
Callistephus (China aster), 22–23, 43
Calluna (Scotch heather), 24–25
  drying, *48,* 49
  as filler, 63
Camellia (Camellia), 24–25
Campanula (Bellflower), 24–25, *61*
Candytuft. *See Iberis*
Cape jasmine. *See Gardenia*
Carnation. *See Dianthus caryophyllus*
Catkins, as filler, 63
Cattails, preserving, 47–48
Centaurea cyanus (Cornflower, Bachelor's button), 12, *24,* 24–25
  in hand-tied bouquet, 86, *86–87*
  for Old Masters bouquet, 73
Centerpieces. *See* Dinner table arrangements
Chaenomeles (Flowering quince), 9, 24–25, 47
Cherry. *See Prunus*
Chicken wire, *52,* 54

China aster. *See Callistephus*
Chincherinchee. *See Ornithogalum*
Chinese flower arranging, 5
Choosing flowers, 62–64, 71
Christmas arrangements, *11,* 11–12, *56*
Chrysanthemum species, *10,* 11
  C. frutescens (Marguerite), 19, 24–25, *72, 73*
  C. maximum (Shasta daisy), 24–25
  C. × morifolium (Florist's chrysanthemum), 24–25
  as focal materials, 63
  foliage decay, 43
  microwave drying, 51
  preconditioning treatment, 44
Citric acid, 46
Cleaning glycerinated plants, 52
Clematis (Clematis), 24–25
  for parallel cluster, 91
  preserving seed heads, 48
  removing foliage, 43
Cluster bouquet, *88–89,* 89, 91
Cocktail party arrangements, 12
Coleus, 90–91, *90–91*
Color, 64–66
  in all-white floral sculpture, 74, *75*
  background considerations, 68
  balance with, 63
  in dried arrangements, 85
  glycerinating changes, 52
  in landscape arrangement, 90–91, *90–91*
  in spring tulip bouquet, 80–81, *82–83*
Color wheel, 65, *67*
Columbine (*Aquilegia*), 22–23, 78
Complementary harmony, 65, *66*
Composition, 64
Conditioning flowers, 43–45
  tulips after shipping, 80
  water additives, 46
Coneflower. *See Rudbeckia*
Cones, 38, 55
Consolida (Larkspur, Annual delphinium), 24–25, *62, 84,* 85
Containers, 53, 69
  for cluster bouquet, *88–89,* 89
  context and, 68
  for country-style arrangement, *76,* 77

galvanized tub, 80, *81*
  growing in, 19, 20
  for landscape arrangement, 90
  for moribana arrangement, 78
  moving, 20
  for Old Masters dried arrangement, 85
  practical considerations, 53
  proportion rules, 63–64
  for rose bouquet, 80
  silver bowl, *82–83*
  for spring tulip bouquet, 80–81, *82–83*
  as starting point, 71
  sterilizing, 46
  texture, 69
  transferring flowers to, 45
  unglazed, protecting furniture from, 53
Context. *See* Setting
Contrasting textures, 67
Convallaria (Lily-of-the-valley), *24,* 24–25, 64
Coral bells (*Heuchera sanguinea*), 30–31
Cordyline terminalis (Ti), 24–25
Coreopsis (Coreopsis), 12, 24–25
  for ikebana, 78
  for Old Masters bouquet, 73
Corkscrew willow. *See Salix matsudana* 'Tortuosa'
Cornflower. *See Centaurea cyanus*
Cornus (Dogwood), 24–25
  forcing, 47
  for ikebana, 78
  microwave drying, 51
Corsages, 55, *56,* 57
Cosmos (Cosmos), *17, 24,* 24–25, 89
Country-style arrangement, 68, *76,* 77
Cow parsnip, 11, 47
Crabapple (*Malus*), 32–33, 47
Crape myrtle, 9
Crataegus (Hawthorn), 24–25, 47, *72,* 73
Crown imperial (*Fritillaria imperialis*), 28–29
Cutting branches, 46
Cutting flowers, 42, 53
Cutting garden, 19–20, 21
  choosing plants for, 22–37
  mail-order sources for, 55
Cyclamens, 11

D

Daffodil. *See Narcissus*
Dahlia (Dahlia), *26,* 26–27
  balance with, 63

drying in sand, 50
  as focal materials, 63
  foliage decay, 43
  for ikebana, 78
  preconditioning steps, 44
Daisies
  dessicant-drying, *50*
  as focal materials, 63
  in Fourth of July arrangements, 12
  gathering, 41
  for landscape arrangement, 91
  Michaelmas. *See* Aster
  Shasta. *See Chrysanthemum × maximum*
Daphne (Daphne), 19, 26–27, 47
Daylily. *See Hemerocallis*
Delphinium (Delphinium), 17, 26–27, *71*
  in dried arrangement, 51
  drying, 49
  for landscape arrangement, 91
  preconditioning steps, 44
Delphinium, annual. *See Consolida*
Desert candle. *See Eremurus*
Desert penstemon. *See Penstemon*
Design, 59–69
  with air-drying flowers, 49
  context. *See* Setting
  with dried flowers, 47, *84,* 85
  with glycerinated plants, 52
  with preserved flowers, 47
  starting point, 71
  using mechanics, 54–55
Dessication, 48, 49–50
Dianthus
  D. barbatus (Sweet William), 26–27
  D. caryophyllus (Carnation), 26–27, 51, 63, 78
  D. deltoides (Pinks), 19, 26–27
Digitalis (Foxglove), 26, 26–27
  in country-style arrangement, *76,* 77
  in nursery arrangement, 14–15
  in Old Masters bouquet, *72,* 73
Dill, *12,* 49, *70*
Dinner table arrangements, 12, *12,* 16, *88–89,* 89
Distilled water, 46
Dock, 47

Dogwood. See Cornus
Dominance, 63
Dried arrangements, 84, 85
  floral foam for, 52
  gathering flowers for, 47–48
  setting for, 68
Dried foliage, 26–27, 30–31, 38, 48
Driftwood, 38
Dusty miller, 42, 43, 44
Dutch iris. See Iris

E
Easter arrangements, 12
Echinops (Globe thistle), 26, 26–27
Eggplant, 90–91, 90–91
Egyptian flower uses, 5
Elderberries, 62
English iris. See Iris
English ivy. See Hedera helix
Entryway arrangements, 16
Equipment. See Tools and equipment
Equisetum (Horsetail), 47, 86, 86–87, 91
Eremurus (Foxtail lily, Desert candle), 26–27, 62, 74
Erica (Heath), 26–27
Eryngium (Sea holly), 26–27, 78
Eucalyptus pulverulenta (Eucalyptus), 26–27, 49, 51
Euphorbia pulcherrima (Poinsettia), 11, 26–27, 44
European influence
  in country-style arrangement, 76, 77
  in hand-tied bouquet, 86, 86–87
  in mass arrangements, 60
  in Old Masters arrangements, 6, 7, 72, 73, 84, 85
Evergreens, 9, 11, 11–12
Exotic plants, buying, 21

F
False spiraea. See Astilbe
Fennel, 38, 66
  drying, 49
  gathering, 47
Ferns, 19, 26–27
  conditioning, 44
  in country-style arrangement, 76, 77
  for landscape arrangement, 91
  in summer arrangements, 11
Fig, 90–91, 90–91

Filler materials, 63
  dried, 84, 85
Flamingo flower. See Anthurium
Flax leaf, 68
Fleabane, for parallel cluster, 91
Floral foam, 40, 52, 54
  in country-style arrangement, 76, 77
  cutting, 53
  in landscape arrangement, 90
  in Old Masters bouquet, 73
  in Old Masters dried arrangement, 85
  plugging hollow stems with, 44
  preventing from drying, 46
  in spring tulip bouquet, 80
  in summer rose bouquet, 80
Floral supplies, 40, 52, 53–55
Floral tape, 40, 52
Florist flowers, 11–12, 21, 43
Florists, 19, 19, 20–21, 43
Florist's chrysanthemum. See Chrysanthemum × morifolium
Florist's clay, 52, 54
Florist's scissors, 40, 42, 46, 53
Florist's tape, 54
Florist's wire, 54–55
Flossflower, 49
Flowering branches, forcing, 46–47
Flowering cherry; Flowering plum. See Prunus
Flowering quince. See Chaenomeles
Flowering tobacco. See Nicotiana
Focal flowers, 62–63
  in dried arrangement, 84, 85
  in ikebana, 78, 79
Foliage
  in country-style arrangement, 76, 77
  fuzzy, 42, 44, 45
  gathering for preserving, 48
  glycerinating, 52–53
  preventing decay in, 42, 44, 45
  removing from drying flowers, 49
  in seasonal arrangements, 9, 11
  submerging during conditioning, 44
Forcing branches, 46–47
Forget-me-not. See Myosotis

Form, 60–64
  in all-white floral sculpture, 74, 75
  background considerations, 68
Forsythia (Forsythia), 26–27
  forcing, 47
  in ikebana, 78–79, 78
  as line material, 62
Found materials, 38
Fourth of July arrangements, 12
Foxglove. See Digitalis
Foxtail lily. See Eremurus
Fragrance, growing flowers for, 19, 21, 22–37
Freesia (Freesia), 26–27
  in Christmas wedding arrangements, 56
  in cluster bouquet, 88–89, 89
  in garden arrangement, 17
  in informal arrangement, 70
  in Old Masters bouquet, 72, 73
  for sculptural arrangement, 74
Fritillaria imperialis (Crown imperial), 28–29
Fruit, 38
  in Christmas wedding arrangements, 56
  as focal materials, 62
  in landscape arrangement, 90–91, 90–91
Fruit tree branches, forcing, 47
Fuchsia (Fuchsia), 28–29, 90–91, 90–91
Fungi, 38
Fuzzy foliage, 42, 44, 45

G
Gaillardia (Blanket flower), 12, 28–29, 43
Galax, 86, 86–87
Galls, 38
Garden arrangements, 17, 90–91, 90–91
Gardenia (Gardenia, Cape jasmine), 19, 28–29
  conditioning, 44
  contrasting textures in, 67
Gardening tips, 19–20, 21. See also Gathering
Garlands
  Christmas, 11
  historical use of, 5
  making, 55, 57
  on stairway, 7
Gathering
  flowering branches, 46

fresh flowers, 41–43
  for preserving, 48–49, 52–53
Gayfeather. See Liatris
Genista, 84, 85
Geranium. See Pelargonium
Gerbera (Gerbera, Transvaal daisy), 28–29, 63
  in country-style arrangement, 76, 77
  in summer arrangement, 9
Geum (Geum), 28–29
Ginger, buying from florists, 21
Gladiolus (Gladiolus), 28, 28–29
  conditioning, 45
  gathering, 41
  as line material, 62
Glass containers, 68, 69, 75
Globe amaranth. See Gomphrena
Globe thistle. See Echinops
Gloriosa (Gloriosa lily, Glory lily), 19, 28–29
Gloves, 40
Glycerine preserving, 48, 51, 52–53
Gomphrena (Globe amaranth), 28–29
Gourds, 11, 53
Grains, 48
Grape hyacinth. See Muscari
Grasses
  in dried arrangement, 47
  drying, 49
  as filler, 63
  gathering 47, 48
  for ikebana, 78
  in informal arrangement, 70
  in nursery arrangement, 14–15
  for Old Masters bouquet, 72, 73
  for texture, 67
Gravel, 55
Great Britain, influence of, 7
Greek flower use, 5
Greenhouse flowers, 19, 21
Grevillea, 90–91, 90–91
Growing flowers. See Gardening tips
Guernsey lily. See Nerine
Gypsophila (Baby's breath), 28–29, 63
Hallway arrangements, 16
Hamamelis (Witch hazel) 28–29, 47
Handling cut flowers, 42–43
Hand-tied bouquet, 86, 86–87

Hardening flowers. See Conditioning
Harmonies, 65
Hawthorn. See Crataegus
Heath (Erica), 26–27
Hedera helix (English ivy), 28–29, 59
Heika style, 78
Helianthus (Sunflower), 28–29, 72, 73
Helichrysum (Strawflower), 28–29
Heliconia (Lobster claw), 28–29
Helleborus (Hellebore), 9, 19, 28–29
Hemerocallis (Daylily), 28, 28–29, 73
Herbs, 11, 20
Heuchera sanguinea (Coral bells), 30–31
Hibiscus rosa-sinensis (Hibiscus), 19, 30–31, 64
Hippeastrum (Amaryllis), 12–13, 30–31
  preconditioning steps, 44
  for sculptural arrangement, 74
History, 5–7, 60
Holiday arrangements, 11–12
Hollow stems, 44
Holly. See Ilex
Hollyhock. See Alcea
Home office arrangement, 16, 16
Honesty. See Lunaria
Horsetail. See Equisetum
Hosta (Hosta, Plantain lily), 11, 30–31, 91
  conditioning, 44
  rhythm with, 64
  texture of, 66
Hyacinth, grape. See Muscari
Hyacinthus (Hyacinth), 9, 30–31
  form and texture, 66
  gathering, 42
  for sculptural arrangement, 74

I
Iberis (Candytuft), 30–31, 43
Iceland poppy. See Papaver nudicaule
Ikebana, 5, 7, 78–79, 78–79
  focal flowers, 63
  form, 60
  proportion rules, 63–64
  starting point, 71
Ilex (Holly), 9, 12, 19, 30, 30–31
Indian corn, 12
Iris, 30–31
  bearded, 30–31, 91
  for cluster bouquet, 89

in country-style arrangement, 76, 77
  as line material, 62
  microwave drying, 51
Ivy, English. See Hedera helix

J
Japanese flower arranging, 5, 7
Japanese maple See Acer palmutum
Jasminus (Jasmine), 9

K
Kalanchoe, 86, 86–87
Kenzan. See Pinholders
Kitchen arrangements, 16
Knife, 52, 53
Kniphofia (Red-hot poker, Torch lily), 30–31
  in landscape arrangement, 90–91, 90–91
Korean flower arranging, 5

L
Landscape arrangement, 90–91, 90–91
Larkspur. See Consolida
Lathyrus (Sweet pea), 30–31
Lavandula (Lavender), 19, 30–31
  in dried arrangement, 84, 85
Leather fern, 76, 77
Leaves, as filler, 63
Liatris (Blazing star, Gayfeather), 30–31, 76, 77
Lichens, 38
Life event celebrations, 9–12
Light, 66, 67, 68
Lilac. See Syringa
Lilium (Lily), 9, 12–13, 17, 30, 30–31, 59
  belladonna lily, in hand-tied bouquet, 86–87
  in cluster bouquet, 89
  in country-style arrangement, 76, 77
  in dried arrangement, 84, 85
  drying with silica gel, 50
  Easter lily, 12, 72, 73
  as focal materials, 63
  for ikebana, 78
  for parallel cluster, 91
  for sculptural arrangement, 74
Lily
  See also Lilium
  foxtail. See Eremurus
  Gloriosa. See Gloriosa
  glory. See Gloriosa
  Guernsey. See Nerine
  plantain. See Hosta
Lily-of-the-Nile. See Agapanthus

Lily-of-the-valley. See Convallaria
Lime soda, 46
Limonium (Statice, Sea lavender), 30, 30–31
  balance with, 63
  in dried arrangement, 84, 85
  for parallel cluster, 91
Line arrangements, 58, 60, 64, 78–79, 78–79
Line-mass arrangements, 60, 61
Line materials, 62
  in dried arrangement, 84, 85
Lobster claw (Heliconia), 28–29
Love-in-a-mist, 72, 73, 78
Lunaria (Money plant, Honesty), 32–33, 67, 72, 73
Lupinus (Lupine), 32–33

M

Madagascar jasmine. See Stephanotis
Magnolia species
  M. grandiflora (Southern magnolia), 19, 32–33, 42, 53
  M. soulangiana (Saucer magnolia), 32–33, 47
  for sculptural arrangement, 74
Mail-order floral supplies, 55
Maintaining arrangements, 41, 45–46
Malus (Apple, Crabapple), 9, 32–33, 47
Mandarin orange, 90–91, 90–91
Maple. See Acer
Marbles, 55
Marguerite. See Chrysanthemum frutescens
Marigold. See Tagetes
Mass arrangements, 60, 62–63
Matthiola (Stock), 32–33
  conditioning, 44
  foliage decay, 43
  for Old Masters bouquet, 72, 73
Meadow grass, 91
Meadowsweet. See Astilbe
Mechanics, 53, 54–55
  in all-white floral sculpture, 74, 75
  in country-style arrangement, 76, 77
  for ikebana, 79
  in landscape arrangement, 90–91

in Old Masters bouquet, 73
in Old Masters dried arrangement, 85
in spring tulip bouquet, 80
in summer rose bouquet, 80
Michaelmas daisy. See Aster
Microwave drying, 50–52, 85
Milky sap, conditioning flowers with, 44
Mock orange. See Philadelphus
Moluccella (Bells of Ireland), 32–33, 42, 49
Money plant. See Lunaria
Monochromatic harmony, 65, 66
Moribana style, 78–79
Mosses, 38, 40, 52
Muscari (Grape hyacinth), 32–33, 44
Myosotis (Forget-me-not), 32–33

N

Nageire style, 79
Narcissus (Daffodil, Narcissus), 19, 32, 32–33
  in Christmas wedding arrangements, 56
  gathering, 42
  growing in containers, 19
  for ikebana, 78
  in parallel composition, 65
  rhythm with, 64
  for sculptural arrangement, 74
  in springtime arrangement, 9
Nasturtium. See Tropaeolum
Nerine (Nerine, Guernsey lily), 32–33, 71
  in florist display, 18
  in garden arrangement, 17
Netting, 54
Nicotiana (Flowering tobacco), 32–33, 74
Nosegays, 56, 57
Nursery arrangement, 14–15

O

Oak (Quercus), 51, 84, 85
Old Masters bouquets, 6, 7, 72, 73
  dried, 84, 85
Orchids, 19, 32–33, 68
  for cluster bouquet, 89
  as focal materials, 63
  microwave drying, 51
  poor man's. See Schizanthus

for sculptural arrangement, 74
Oriental influence, 60, 64. See also Ikebana
Oriental poppy. See Papaver orientale
Ornamental onion. See Allium
Ornithogalum (Star-of-Bethlehem, Chincherinchee), 32–33
  in all-white floral sculpture, 74, 75
  in Christmas wedding arrangements, 56
  in hand-tied bouquet, 86, 86–87
Outdoor florist's shops, 43

P

Paddle wire, 52, 55
Paeonia (Peony), 19, 32, 32–33
  for cluster bouquet, 89
  in dried arrangement, 84, 85
  drying in sand, 50
  as focal flower, 63, 78, 79, 84, 85
  in ikebana, 78–79, 78
  microwave drying, 51
  in nursery arrangement, 14–15
Painted tongue. See Anthurium
Pansy. See Viola × wittrockiana
Papaver species
  for cluster bouquet, 89
  gathering, 41
  for ikebana, 78
  P. nudicaule (Iceland poppy), 34–35, 66
  P. orientale (Oriental poppy), 34–35, 44
  preconditioning, 44
  for sculptural arrangement, 74
Parallel composition, 64, 65, 76, 77, 90, 91
Party arrangements, 12
Peach. See Prunus
Pearly everlasting, 47
Pebbles, 40, 55, 58
Pelargonium (Geranium), 34–35
Penstemon (Penstemon), 34–35
  desert, 90–91, 90–91
Peony. See Paeonia
Peppers, 90–91, 90–91
Persian ranunculus. See Ranunculus
Persimmons, 11, 84, 85
Peruvian daffodils, 78–79, 79
Peruvian lily. See Alstroemeria

Philadelphus (Mock orange), 34–35, 43, 47
Phlox (Phlox), 34–35, 91
Physostegia, 86, 86–87
Pincushion flower. See Scabiosa
Pinholders, 40, 52, 54
Pinks. See Dianthus
Plantain lily. See Hosta
Plum. See Prunus
Poinsettia. See Euphorbia pulcherrima
Poisonous plants, avoiding, 38
Polianthes (Tuberose), 34–35, 74
Pomegranates, 84, 85
Poor man's orchid. See Schizanthus
Poppy. See Papaver
Pot marigold. See Calendula
Preserving cut flowers, 47–53
  air-drying, 49
  with dessicants, 49–50
  with glycerine, 52–53
  by microwave drying, 50–52
  predried plants, 47–48
  preparing for, 48–49, 53
Prickly pear, 90–91, 90–91
Proportion, 63–64, 68
Protea (Protea), 34–35, 67, 68, 78
Pruning shears, 53
Prunus (Plum, Flowering plum, Cherry, Flowering cherry, Peach), 34–35
  forcing, 47, 47
  as line material, 62
Pumpkins, 11, 12
Pussy willow. See Salix caprea

Q

Queen Anne's lace, 38, 47, 49
Quercus (Oak), 51, 84, 85
Quince, 90–91, 90–91
  flowering. See Chaenomeles

R

Radial composition, 64
Rainwater, 46
Ranunculus (Persian ranunculus), 34–35, 78
Recutting forced branches, 46, 47
Red-hot poker. See Kniphofia
Red pepper, 90–91, 90–91
Red salvia, 90–91, 90–91
Refrigerated flowers, 43, 45

Renaissance flower arranging, 7
Rhododendron (Rhododendron), 34–35, 44
Rhythm, 64
Rocks, 38, 58
Roman flower uses, 5
Rosa (Rose), 19, 34–35, 62
  balance with, 63
  buying, 21, 43
  in country-style arrangement, 76, 77
  dessicating, 49, 50
  in dried arrangement, 84, 85
  as focal materials, 63
  gathering, 42
  hybrid tea 'Pristine', 34
  for ikebana, 78
  in informal arrangement, 70
  light and texture, 67
  microwave drying, 51
  red, long-stemmed, 4
  removing thorns, 53
  for sculptural arrangement, 74
  in summer bouquet, 9, 80, 80–81
Rose hips, 90–91, 90–91
Rudbeckia (Coneflower), 12, 34–35, 72, 73, 78
Rushes, 78–79, 79
Rye, 48

S

Salal foliage, 76, 77
Salix species
  S. caprea (Pussy willow), 34, 34–35, 47, 47, 62
  S. matsudana 'Tortuosa' (Corkscrew willow), 34–35, 61, 74, 75
Sand, 50, 55
Saucer magnolia. See Magnolia soulangiana
Scabiosa (Pincushion flower), 36–37
  for ikebana, 78
  for landscape arrangement, 91
  for Old Masters bouquet, 72, 73
Scale, 68
Schizanthus (Poor man's orchid, Butterfly flower), 36–37
Scilla (Bluebell, Squill), 36–37
Scotch heather. See Calluna
Sea holly (Eryngium), 26–27, 78
Sea lavender. See Limonium
Seashells, 38, 55
Seasonal arrangements, 9–12, 90–91

Seaweeds, 38
Secateurs, 53
Sedge, 47
Seed heads, gathering, 48
Setting, 67–68
  for cluster bouquets, 89
  color and, 66
  for country-style arrangement, 76, 77
  for ikebana, 79
  for landscape arrangement, 91
  light and, 66
Shasta daisy. See Chrysanthemum maximum
Silica gel, 49, 50, 51–52
Single blossom, 92, 92
Sitting room arrangements, 12–13, 16
Size, color and, 66
Snapdragon. See Antirrhinum
Snowball (Viburnum), 76, 77
Society garlic, 17
Southern magnolia. See Magnolia grandiflora
Spanish iris. See Iris
Spanish moss, 85
Special-occasion flowers, 56–57
Sphagnum moss, 73, 80
Spiraea (Spiraea), 36–37, 47
Spiraea, false. See Astilbe
Spraying, 46, 52
Springtime arrangements, 9, 42, 80–81, 82–83
Spry, Constance, 7
Squill. See Scilla
Star-of-Bethlehem. See Ornithogalum
Statice. See Limonium
Stems
  cutting for drying, 49
  handling, 42–43
  postconditioning steps, 45
  recutting periodically, 46
  recutting under water, 43, 45
Stephanotis (Madagascar jasmine), 36–37
  in Christmas wedding arrangements, 56
  in garden arrangement, 17
  in informal arrangement, 70
  for sculptural arrangement, 74
Sterilizing tools, 46
Stevia, 62
Stock. See Matthiola
Stokesia (Stokes' aster), 36–37
Storing conditioned flowers, 45

Storing dessicated flowers, 49–50
Storing glycerinated plants, 52
Strawflower. *See Helichrysum*
Strelitzia (Bird-of-paradise), 19, 36–37
Style, 59, 68
Styrofoam, *52*, 54
Sugar, 46, 47
Summer arrangements, 9, *9*, 11, 12, *12*
color considerations, 66
dry-climate landscape, 90–91, *90–91*
hand-tied bouquet, 86, *86–87*
for long vase life, 42
roses, 80, *80–81*
Sunflower. *See Helianthus*
Sweet pea. *See Lathyrus*
Sweet violet. *See Viola odorata*

Sweet William. *See Dianthus barbatus*
Syringa (Lilac), 19, 36–37
in Old Masters bouquet, *72*, 73
removing foliage, 43

T

Tagetes (Marigold), *36*, 36–37
foliage decay, 43
for ikebana, 78
microwave drying, 51
Teasel, 47
Texture, 66–67
in all-white floral sculpture, 74, *75*
background considerations, 68
of container, 69
Thistle, 47. *See also Echinops*
Thorn remover, 53
Ti (*Cordyline terminalis*), *24–25*
Tonic water, 46
Tools and equipment, *40, 52*, 53–55
sterilizing, 46

Torch cactus flower, 92, *92*
Torch lily. *See Kniphofia*
Transvaal daisy. *See Gerbera*
Tropaeolum (Nasturtium), 19, 36–37, 78, 90–91, *90–91*
Tropical arrangements, 12, *68*
Tropical flowers buying, 21
growing, 19
Trumpet plant, *71*
Tuberose. *See Polianthes*
Tulipa (Tulip), 6, 36–37, 80–81, *82–83*
in all-white floral sculpture, 74, *75*
in Christmas wedding arrangements, 56
conditioning, *45*
in country-style arrangement, *76*, 77
as focal materials, 63
greenhouse-grown, 21

for ikebana, 78
microwave drying, 51
in Old Masters bouquet, *72*, 73
rhythm with, 64
setting for, 68

V

Van Huysum, Jan, 6, 85
Vase life maximizing, 43–45, 45–46
selecting flowers for, 42, 43
Vases. *See Containers*
Vase water, 41, 45–46
Vegetables, 11, 12, 38
as focal materials, 62
in landscape arrangement, 90–91, *90–91*
Viburnum (Snowball), *76*, 77
Viola
V. odorata (Sweet violet), 9, 36–37, 91
V. × *wittrockiana* (Pansy), 36–37, 51

W

Water, drying flowers in, 49. *See also* Vase water
Watering can, *52*, 53
Waterproof adhesive tape, 54
Watsonia (Watsonia), *12–13*, 36–37
in country-style arrangement, *76*, 77
in Old Masters bouquet, *72*, 73
for parallel cluster, 91
Wedding arrangements, 12, *56*, 86
Weeds, *14–15*, 47
Wheat, 47, 48
White arrangement, 68, 74, *75*
Wild blackberry, 90–91, *90–91*
Wildflowers, 38, 47, *72*, 73
Windflower. *See Anemone coronaria*
Winter arrangements, 9, *11*, 11–12, *56*, 66

Wire, *52*
Wire cutters, *52*, 53
Wire netting, 54
Wiring flowers, 49, 55
Wisteria (Wisteria), 36–37, 47
Witch hazel. *See Hamamelis*
Wreaths, 11, 55, *56*, 57

Y

Yarrow. *See Achillea*
Zantedeschia (Calla lily), *17*, 36–37
in all-white floral sculpture, 74, *75*
in country-style arrangement, *76*, 77
in Old Masters bouquet, *72*, 73
Zinnia (Zinnia), 36–37, *36*
foliage decay, 43
in Fourth of July arrangements, 12
for Old Masters bouquet, *72*, 73
for sculptural arrangement, 74

U.S. Measure and Metric Measure Conversion Chart

	Symbol	When you know:	Multiply by	To find:	Rounded Measures for Quick Reference		
		Formulas for Exact Measures			**Rounded Measures for Quick Reference**		
Mass (Weight)	oz	ounces	28.35	grams	1 oz		= 30 g
	lb	pounds	0.45	kilograms	4 oz		= 115 g
	g	grams	0.035	ounces	8 oz		= 225 g
	kg	kilograms	2.2	pounds	16 oz	= 1 lb	= 450 kg
					32 oz	= 2 lb	= 900 kg
					36 oz	= 2 1/4 lb	= 1000g (a kg)
Volume	tsp	teaspoons	5.0	milliliters	1/4 tsp	= 1/24 oz	= 1 ml
	tbsp	tablespoons	15.0	milliliters	1/2 tsp	= 1/12 oz	= 2 ml
	fl oz	fluid ounces	29.57	milliliters	1 tsp	= 1/6 oz	= 5 ml
	c	cups	0.24	liters	1 tbsp	= 1/2 oz	= 15 ml
	pt	pints	0.47	liters	1 c	= 8 oz	= 250 ml
	qt	quarts	0.95	liters	2 c (1 pt)	= 16 oz	= 500 ml
	gal	gallons	3.785	liters	4 c (1 qt)	= 32 oz	= 1 l
	ml	milliters	0.034	fluid ounces	4 qt (1 gal)	= 128 oz	= 3 3/4·l
Length	in.	inches	2.54	centimeters	3/8 in.	= 1 cm	
	ft	feet	30.48	centimeters	1 in.	= 2.5 cm	
	yd	yards	0.9144	meters	2 in.	= 5 cm	
	mi	miles	1.609	kilometers	2-1/2 in.	= 6.5 cm	
	km	kilometers	0.621	miles	12 in. (1 ft)	= 30 cm	
	m	meters	1.094	yards	1 yd	= 90 cm	
	cm	centimeters	0.39	inches	100 ft	= 30 m	
					1 mi	= 1.6 km	
Temperature	°F	Fahrenheit	5/9 (after subtracting 32)	Celsius	32°F	= 0°C	
	°C	Celsius	9/5 (then add 32)	Fahrenheit	68°F	= 20°C	
					212°F	= 100°C	
Area	in.²	square inches	6.452	square centimeters	1 in.²	= 6.5 cm²	
	ft²	square feet	929.0	square centimeters	1 ft²	= 930 cm²	
	yd²	square yards	8361.0	square centimeters	1 yd²	= 8360 cm²	
	a	acres	0.4047	hectares	1 a	= 4050 m²	